A TAUPO FISHING DIARY

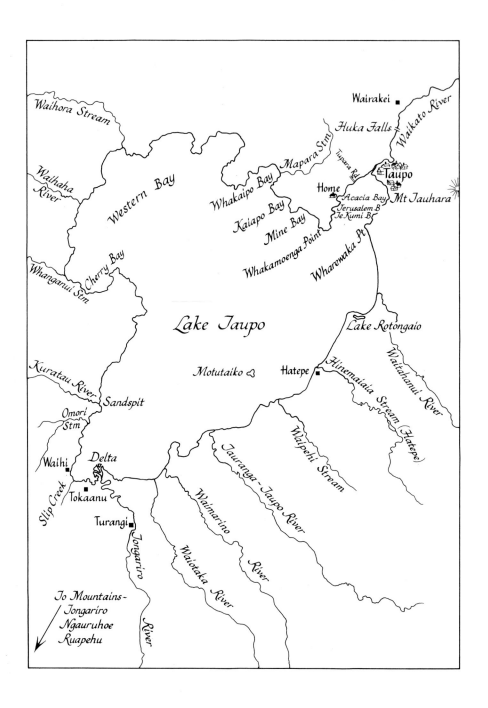

A Taupo Fishing Diary

ALEX GILLETT

Illustrated by JANE PERRY

HODDER AND STOUGHTON
AUCKLAND LONDON SYDNEY

Text copyright © 1981 Alex Gillett.
Illustrations © 1981 Jane Perry.
First published 1981.
ISBN 0 340 26951 0

Typeset by Linotype Service (P.N.) Limited, Palmerston North
Printed and bound in Hong Kong for Hodder & Stoughton Ltd, 44-46 View
Road, Glenfield, Auckland, New Zealand.

For Judy Turner

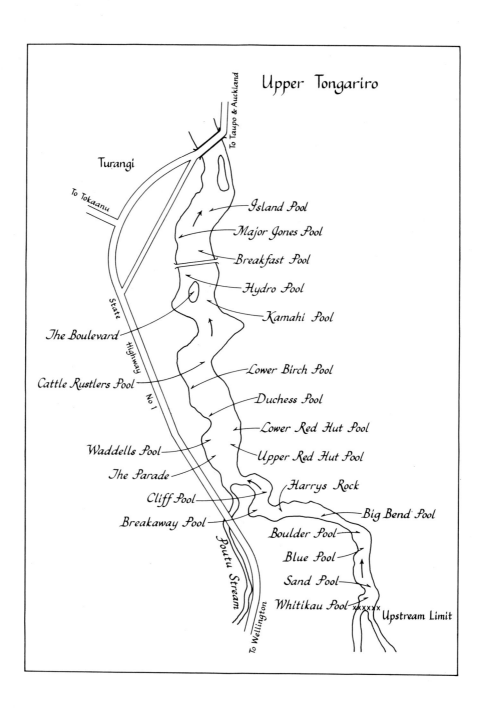

Upper Tongariro

To Taupo & Auckland

Turangi

To Tokaanu

State Highway No 1

Island Pool

Major Jones Pool

Breakfast Pool

Hydro Pool

Kamahi Pool

The Boulevard

Lower Birch Pool

Cattle Rustlers Pool

Duchess Pool

Lower Red Hut Pool

Waddells Pool

Upper Red Hut Pool

The Parade

Harrys Rock

Cliff Pool

Big Bend Pool

Breakaway Pool

Boulder Pool

Blue Pool

Sand Pool

Poutu Stream

Whitikau Pool

Upstream Limit

To Wellington

Foreword

Alex Gillett is a man for all seasons with the talent to appreciate, enjoy and record the changing face of nature as the year runs its course. This book is basically the diary of a fisherman, but it is much more than that. It is a chronicle of the joys of the simple life of a man and his wife and their home on the shores of Lake Taupo, their garden and how it grows, their enigmatic cat and their irrepressible dog, their friends, from far and near, who call in and enjoy their fine food and good music or go fishing together. Throughout the year he observes the trees and the flowers, and the bird, animal and insect life which abounds round the lake.

Through the daily recording of this gentle life runs the tight line of the angler who knows and loves Lake Taupo with all its changing moods and challenges. No other place in New Zealand or perhaps anywhere else on earth provides such variety of trout fishing as this lake and the rivers and streams which flow into it. I have fished there for over a quarter of a century from the headwaters of the Waiotaka to the shelving beach at the mouth of the Waihaha and from the Western Bays to that magnificent river, which my children, who have grown up with a fishing rod in their hands, call 'the mighty Tonga'.

I know Taupo fishing mainly at Christmas and Easter, the only times I could get away from the chains of office, but Alex Gillett knows it from day to day through the year and from year to year. There is not much that he does not know about trout and their ways and in this diary he imparts his angler's lore in the humorous, vivid and lively way that true fishermen do when they relax in the evening after a strenuous day on the river.

7

The value of this book is enhanced by the charming illustrations with which Jane Perry has embellished its pages. The birds, animals and insects, the trees and the flowers, the Taupo scenes and, of course, the trout have been drawn and painted with careful precision and with an artist's eye for form and colour which complement the printed word and enlarge the reader's appreciation of the story.

I was especially interested in the illustrations of the flies — the ones we fish with. They have been painstakingly portrayed in all their colourful glory. Flies are the subject of endless discussion among anglers. My own preference is for fishing up the smaller streams where I can see and stalk the trout, with a Green Beetle or a nymph and then come back downstream casting into the pools with a Parson's Glory or a Red Setter. Jane Perry's range of illustrations and Alex Gillett's descriptions of many encounters, enticing the elusive trout with so many different flies, will enlarge the vision and raise the hopes of the fishermen who are fortunate enough to read this book.

Sir John Marshall, 1981.

Lake Taupo

LAKE TAUPO, the largest body of fresh water in New Zealand, lies about 350 metres above sea level on the North Island's high volcanic plateau.

It covers 600 square kilometres and is nearly forty kilometres long and twenty-seven kilometres across at its widest part.

The lake lies over a series of craters and was formed by volcanic subsidence many thousands of years ago. The surrounding region still contains much thermal activity, including the Wairakei thermal borefield, which has been developed to tap underground super-heated steam for the generation of electric power.

More than 650 kilometres of river feed the lake, draining an area of 3,000 square kilometres. The main one of these is the Tongariro, which flows in at the southern end and comes out where the township of Taupo is located at the northern end as the start of the Waikato. The Waikato is New Zealand's longest river and supports a number of hydro-electric stations.

South of the lake stand the still active volcanoes of Ruapehu (2,797 metres) and Ngauruhoe (2,291 metres), and the dormant Tongariro crater complex (1,968 metres). To the east are the densely bushed Kaimanawa Ranges.

Lake Taupo and its rivers are generally recognised as comprising the most consistent rainbow trout fishery in the world.

The Maoris of the Taupo region, the Ngati Tuwharetoa, claim descent from the tohunga Ngatoroirangi of the Te Arawa canoe, one of the fleet of seven that tradition says arrived in New Zealand from Hawaiki in the 14th century.

The navigator of the Te Arawa canoe, Tia, was another forebear of the tribe, whose travels, like those of Ngatoroirangi, brought him to the Taupo area, but by another route. The full name of the lake is *Taupo-nui-a-Tia,* 'the Great Shoulder Mat of Tia'.

With their followers, the two men went their separate ways after the New Zealand landfall but both came eventually to Taupo. The Ngati Tuwharetoa legend tells that Ngatoroirangi, searching for land in which to settle his followers, came to the summit of Mount Tauhara. Before him lay a great empty dustbowl. He plucked a totara tree from the mountain and hurled it into the dustbowl. Its branches pierced the earth, and water welled up to form Taupo Moana, the Sea of Taupo. The tohunga then plucked strands from his cloak and threw two of them into the water, where they became the genesis of the lake's native fish, the kokupu and the inanga. He threw in a third strand which became an eel, but it wriggled only a few yards and died.

Today there are no eels in Lake Taupo and there is no evidence to suggest there ever have been.

Ngatoroirangi is also credited with having brought fire to the volcanic peaks of Ruapehu, Ngauruhoe and Tongariro.

This is the version of the lake's creation which I prefer.

Alex Gillett.

September

Acacia Bay

September 1

The first day of spring officially, but not really what I would have hoped for.

This morning a chill northerly hustled the whitecaps down the lake and roared in the pines behind the house. I felt I should make an effort to mark the turn of the seasons and spent two hours at Whakamoenga Rocks before lunch. The northerly passes overhead here, but I could see it and hear it, thrashing the trees around the cottage above the point.

I fished close to the navigation light for half an hour, searching the deep water with a Yellow Rabbit on a fast-sinking line. No response so I moved along to the flat outcrop on the right. Again the lure probed deep along the shelving rocks and on the third cast came up against something solid. The fish fought deep and stubbornly at first but soon came to the net, a spawned-out jack, still dark and rather thin, who would have weighed 5½lb in his prime.

Yellow Rabbit

I unhooked him in the net then lowered it under the water and watched him wobble away into the depths.

An hour later the wind had freshened and moved a few points to the west, driving cold onto my right cheek. Nothing else had touched the lure. I walked back through the bush past the old Maori cave and climbed the track between the close growing manuka and five finger to the car. Driving back along the Acacia Bay Road, the wind spattered the first drops of rain on the windscreen and by the time I reached home it was coming down steadily.

Not an inspiring start to spring but there must be better days ahead. The wind has dropped now but the rain continues with soft intensity. It's a little warmer than it has been, but the fire is still welcome.

September 4

A mouldy grey sort of a day again, gusting northerlies with intermittent rain. Gave the big vegetable bed another turning over, dug in rotted fowl manure and spread a blanket of bush compost. Carrots can go in any day now. We spent an hour or so this evening drawing a planting and sowing plan and sorting out seed packets.

September 5

Wharewaka Point never treats me very well and today was no exception. Sometimes when the smelt are running later in the year I take the odd fish but I don't often go there. Too close to the main road and easy to fish from the gently sloping pumice beach. And there are houses close by — a social fisherman I am not.

At ten o'clock this morning the sun was trying hard but the persistent northerly kept a scatter of cloud across its face. Two other anglers there and one beached a bright little maiden fish as I arrived. Hooked two fish, small ones I think, in the first forty minutes and lost them both within seconds. Casting automatically after a while and looking across the lake at Acacia Bay I could see the house and wondered what Nick was doing. We'd bought a weeping willow and two silver birches yesterday and perhaps she was out planting them, but it was too far to see.

Silver birches are probably my favourite tree, I was thinking, when a violent pull jerked me awake. I leaned back on the rod and a fish leapt only twenty feet in front of me, slapped back onto the water and came off. Had one more strike during the next twenty minutes and decided to call it a day. I'd promised to be home by twelve.

The wind was gusting strongly now, slapping waves high up my waders. Clouds had gathered in the north and a dark solid bank spread towards the lake. This time I reached home just before the rain.

Nick had just finished planting the trees.

'Well, where is it?' she asked. 'I was expecting one for dinner tonight.'

I cocked a thumb over my shoulder at the lake. 'That's where it is. It didn't want to come home for dinner.'

'Then it's just as well I took one out of the deep-freeze last night, isn't it?' She smiled complacently.

September 8

Grey and cold still but there must be an improvement soon. Put in an hour on the garden. Carrots sown now and tomatoes seeded in the sunporch.

September 11

A better day than we've had for a while. Spent an hour and a half this morning off the groin at the end of Tupara Road fishing the shallow water with a floating line and small Hamill's Killer. Hooked four fish but landed only two. The best one, well over 4lb, came home for the freezer.

A pair of mallard with their five early youngsters were holding swimming and follow-my-leader lessons between the two groins. The last ball of fluff in the queue kept falling behind and having to do miracles of water-walking to catch up. A harrier, riding the high thermals on ragged wings, circled above us for half an hour then took off inland. I've never yet seen one stoop over water, but I suppose he thought they might go ashore if he waited long enough.

Perhaps I stopped them coming in. They were still on the water when I left and Tail-end Charlie seemed to be keeping up much better already.

September 14

Tired and aching all over, but I don't care, it was a great day.

The Tongariro's in lovely order now, running bright and clear after last week's rain.

The sun was warm today but not yet strong enough to melt the snow on the triple peaks. Ngauruhoe trailed a brown plume to the south, dark against the powder-blue sky. We don't get many early spring days like this. The river clamped the waders cold against my legs in the long broken run half a mile below the Cliff Pool. I began to cast the fat caddis nymph up into the pale green channels between the boulders and the white line slid back fast along the surface.

Worked slowly upstream for half an hour, missing a strike in the lee of a midstream rock. Stumbling and slipping against the river's thrust, I dropped the nymph in the smooth glide beside a fallen pine. The line stopped, the rod arched and a good fish thrashed on the surface then powered upstream into white water taking all the casting line in one run. It held in the current for a few moments then came tumbling downstream peeling off backing, forcing me to follow, slipping and floundering over the greasy rocks. Eventually beached it on a gravel bar close in to the high bank, a fresh-run hen of 5½lb, plump and silver from the lake. I buried her in a cocoon of fern and long grass and marked the place with a stick. Then I climbed the bank and sat with my legs hanging over. A fantail wheeled and pirouetted in the manuka beside me. They enjoy human company these delicate little birds — especially when you disturb insects from the foliage.

Above the muted roar of the river a magpie gargled from the big macrocarpa on the far side. One for sorrow I thought. Then its mate alighted on a higher branch. Two for joy — that's better. Above my head the golden toi-toi flags waved and fell in the new breeze.

Took two more fish in the broad heavy water of the Cliff, smaller than the first but both fresh-run and they went back for another day. Then on to the tail of the pool below Boulder Reach. Two men were fishing the far side with lures. Each had taken a fish, they told me, but much earlier that morning.

The nymph worked through the deep water under the flax and toi-toi on my side but nothing came. I reeled in and started the forty-minute walk back to the Red Hut Pool and the car, picking up the hidden fish on the way. My face was tingling from the unaccustomed sun and every joint was stiff.

They still are, but I don't care. Beautiful river, beautiful fish.

September 16

Wind hell-bent from the south today, blasting up from the cold mountains at the far end of the lake. We miss most of it here in Acacia Bay but this morning we watched the long white combers pounding onto Wharewaka Point on the other side and a launch rolling and lurching back to harbour from an unwise early start.

Took the trailer out towards Whakamoenga Point to dig leaf compost in the bush, and we heard the boom and slap of the waves on the rocks from almost half a mile away.

Noticed Acacia Bay was relatively calm on the way back so tried there for an hour this afternoon. But there was heavy swell and this southerly can blow round corners. Twice hooked the poplars on my backcast and left them one fly. No fish, just wind.

It's late now and the wind is gusting intermittently. I think its going down, although they often last for two or three days.

September 17

I was half right. Southerly has eased but it hasn't finished yet. Colder than yesterday, strangely enough, despite the slackening of the wind.

Took two fish in the deep water off Acacia Bay Point late this afternoon. One went back and the other is in the oven now, wrapped in tinfoil. Stuffed with breadcrumbs, grated onion and orange peel, a sprig of rosemary and a knob of butter. And there'll be fresh broccoli from the garden to go with it.

September 20

It felt like a Whakaipo day when I woke up this morning.

Last week's southerly has wasted away and a gentle breeze puffed high fleecy cumulus out of the north-west. Not a good wind for Whakaipo but you can never quite tell until you get there — or I can't anyway.

The poplars above the stream mouth were shivering their new leaves and the sun kindled sparks from the wavelets across the broad expanse of the bay. To the right the mile-long pumice beach stretched in a smooth curve to the cliff at the far end and the waves whispered quietly all along the shore. A pair of mallard rose up from the stream mouth, whirring out onto the lake with anxious haste.

Most people favour the stream mouth but I've never had great success there during daylight. I walked ankle-deep around to the left where the big willow stands at the far end of the little bay. The willows will soon be in leaf but now their thin burnt-orange arms stand out brightly against the drab manuka. Fished back from the big willow, casting easily with the breeze on my left shoulder. I know just about every rock and hole in this bay and my slow sideways two-step takes a little more than half an hour to bring me back to the stream mouth.

Struck nothing this time so waded along the rocky foreshore towards my favourite place half a mile round from the stream. The tiny bay is only about forty yards across and the bush comes right down to the water's edge when the lake's at normal height. Blackbirds and warblers sing in the bush and sometimes I see a shining cuckoo. A twisted peach tree blossoms here every year but I never see fruit. I suppose the opossums beat me to it. Wading out to clear the trees for my backcast, the small Hairy Dog drops into the centre of the bay. At the fourth or fifth cast a heavy pull dips the rod point and the line zips out towards the middle of the lake. Far out — it seems halfway across — the fish leaps high. I slowly recover backing and line until another powerful run strips the reel again. Then after quite a long time the lovely silver-pink hen lies shining on the stones of the beach.

Took another from the far side of the bay, a 4-pounder which came ashore almost as unwillingly as the first. Then I slipped the baling twine through their gills, tied it around

Hairy Dog

17

my waist and waded back towards the stream. The stream
bay was calm now so I continued back to the car. Another
car was parked beside it and a young man and his wife
admired the fish. 'I've heard this stream mouth's good,' he
told me as he examined the fly. 'So that's what you get them
on is it? Afraid I've got nothing like that.'

On an impulse I bit off the Hairy Dog and handed it to
him. 'There you are, have a go with that. But you don't
have to stick to the mouth you know. There's plenty of
good water all along there past the big willow.'

September 22

Fired up the smoker this morning. The day before
yesterday's Whakaipo brace went in, together with four that
George took trolling in Mine Bay the same day.
Well-smoked trout is fit only for royalty and anglers, but
sometimes one should allow lesser mortals the chance to
taste it just to show them what they're missing.

I split the fish down the backbone from inside, lay them
flat and pat in a mixture of two parts coarse salt to one part
brown sugar. Some sybarites use honey instead of sugar but
I feel this is an unnecessary extravagance. They lie flat
overnight to absorb the mixture then hang by the 'wings' to
drip-dry for some hours. I make a smother of manuka
sawdust and hang them well above the heat. If they're too
close they cook rather than smoke and don't last as long.

Twelve hours does the trick but a little longer if the weather is humid.

Today's work will be tested tomorrow. It's a long time to wait but I think it'll be worth it.

September 23

George collected his smoked fish and departed with almost indecent haste this morning.

We waited until lunchtime, then I applied myself to the 6-pounder, lifting the ribs and backbone to reveal creamy pink flesh beneath. I eased it away from the skin and placed the two large fillets on a dish. Nick made open sandwiches of wholemeal bread and sprinkled them with lemon juice and fresh-ground black pepper. And to think some people pay a fortune for smoked salmon!

For breakfast tomorrow I'll simmer a piece in milk, but Nick prefers it *au naturel*.

Over-indulgence in smoked trout carries its own penalties, as my friend Kevin knows only too well. He and I were staying with Ken one summer weekend in his house on the mouth of the Ngongotaha River, which flows into Lake Rotorua. Kevin is a fanatical fisherman. To be unable to fish while others do is for him to peer over the inner rim of Hell.

At that time in that place the trout came on to feed after dark. We were preparing our gear that evening, rigging up rods, comparing lures and getting out the body waders against the witching hour.

Kevin held up a Scotch Poacher to the last of the sunset. 'Now you know and I know,' he said, 'that this fly will take a limit bag tonight.' Ken had completed a batch of trout in his smoker the previous day and Kevin had been sampling the goods during the afternoon and also had some for dinner. He was a great one for smoked trout. Before preparing himself for the night's fishing, he'd paid another trip to the larder. Now he climbed laboriously into his

Scotch Poacher

waders. As he made the final adjustments to the shoulder straps a pained look crossed his face and he quickly began to disrobe. In no time at all his protective gear was lying at his feet and he made off at a swift trot towards the house. He reappeared ten minutes later looking a trifle drawn and began to climb back into the waders.

It was now completely dark and Ken and myself were ready to start fishing. Again, as he made the final adjustments to his waders, the same pained look crossed Kevin's face. With admirable speed he again disrobed and ran off to the house yelping and muttering to himself. We made our way to the river mouth and waded in.

Later I looked over my shoulder to see a shadowy figure once more manfully struggling into waders and parka. This time everything seemed to be alright and he soon joined us in the river. He'd barely begun to strip line from his reel when he gave an agonised grunt and started to back-pedal out of the water. Stumbling ashore he tore off his gear and disappeared into the darkness. Three more times that night he tried to join us but he never got beyond the first cast.

When we came in at eleven o'clock, Kevin was standing mournfully on the beach. His malady at last seemed to have run its course. Ken and myself had six good fish between us, one of them an 8lb brownie. I conclude from this that while a little of what you fancy does you good, you can also have too much of a good thing!

September 26

'We've no rabbits left,' Nick told me last night. She was a bit flushed from rummaging around in the bottom of the deep-freeze.

'Perhaps we ought to breed them,' I suggested. 'But then of course you couldn't eat them if they were members of the family.'

But I took the point, and this morning before daylight I took the .22 up through the pines and into the scrub on the

20

hill behind the house. It was cold and clear and there were stars still in the west. I spread the oilskin parka at the edge of the scrub and scanned the fenceline through the 'scope. Nothing moved so I shivered for ten minutes then looked again. A white and pallid sun lifted beyond Tauhara, silvering the wet grass of the paddock and suddenly there was a rabbit squatting beside the fence fifty yards to my left. I eased around, centred the cross-hairs on the shoulder and squeezed one off. The rabbit dropped and lay without a quiver. When I picked it up I found the Hornet had taken it clean through the head. I told Nick later that I'd aimed for the head to avoid spoiling the meat!

September 28

The upper Waitahanui ran dark and cold this morning, sliding fast and black under the manuka overhang.

When I crossed the main highway bridge before sunrise, two vague figures stood chest-deep below the bridge and another above. Probably at least six or seven others were working the rip where the river angles into the lake but it was too dark to see. I turned down Blake Road and drove to the end, then walked upriver to the grass flats, still crisp and white from the night's frost.

In the swift run under the far bank, the white line stopped in its drift and five minutes later I twisted the Half-back nymph from the jaw of a thin 3-pounder and returned her to the water. Now the eastern hills were stark black against the orange flush of the rising sun and the fantails began hawking early flies above the grass.

Soon the river changed to metallic grey, shot with white in the strong water. Hooked and lost another fish under the flax, then landed a heavy-shouldered 4lb jack from the fast water at the head of the pool. Fresh from the lake, a late runner at this time of year, he took me down the rapids and into the tail of the next pool before I could get the net under him. The sun had lifted from the hills by now and the morning sky was cold pale blue. A fish snapped off the nymph in the broken water between two pools. Tied on another and fished up the next three pools without a touch. Then I hefted the 4-pounder back to the car. Three rods above the bridge when I drove back and two below. Further on, nine others were strung across the rip. As I passed, one rod lifted in a kicking arc and a fish boiled on the shining surface of the lake.

Waitahanui

October

Mission Bay

October 1

It really is getting warmer. Nick hasn't used the electric blanket for three nights now and Herman has been staying out later than usual. Last night he had a hellish wailing match with some neighbouring cat. We looked out to see them sitting in the moonlight on the lawn hurling abuse at each other from a distance of six feet. They were still going spasmodically when we went to bed. Later, there was a thump on the sundeck then a crescendo of cursing followed by silence. We heard Herman scrabble through the top window and drop to the floor inside. He may not be strong on valour but no-one could fault his discretion.

October 3

Spring has really woken up the garden now. The new silver birches are greening up beautifully. Lovely trees, even bare of leaves standing against a powder-blue winter sky.

Tomato plants are doing nicely in the sunporch too, hairy mauve stems curving towards the sun. They'll be planted out in about four weeks. Labour Day, the experts say, but I'm always a bit wary of late frosts at this elevation.

Whakaipo tomorrow if the weather's right. It's two weeks since I was there. I'm ordering a light southerly to bring a ripple into the bay, and some bright sunshine. A shower or two will be welcome — this always seems to help.

October 4

Well, not quite what I'd ordered really. The southerly didn't show up on time and from the Mapara Road just after eight in the morning the bay looked blue and satin-smooth. Hopeless for fishing, but who can resist driving down to have a look? I can't.

Mapara Stream was in good heart, pushing a rusty finger straight out into the left-hand corner of the bay. The sun had followed orders at least and there was feathery cirrus high in the west. I stood back from the mouth and flicked the small Hairy Dog just beyond the gravel bar only inches from the

bank and let it ride the current. There's often a fish lying in close here. Tried again twice more but no-one was home.

The lake is high at present which meant wading deep around the fallen tree to the left of the stream mouth, catching my net on a projecting knob as usual. Past the big willow the only thing moving was a heron, carefully stalking cockabullies in the sun-dappled shallows. He allowed me thirty yards leeway before lifting from the water and beating slowly back towards the stream mouth. His prospects were probably far better than mine. Nothing else moved apart from a black shag cruising far out and the golden motes of pollen floating in the still air.

I sloshed and stumbled over the slippery rocks to my favourite small bay well on from the stream mouth. An hour later the Hairy Dog had dried out completely. Waded slowly back, pushing ripples out onto the smooth water. The pale wash of the willows' early green stands out against the burnt brown of the manuka behind. Not a fish to be seen, not a sign of a rise. I wasn't too concerned. The other rewards of a spring morning are enough. Late now, and the southerly has arrived with a vengeance. We miss most of it here in Acacia Bay, but I can hear it tearing at the tops of the pines in the darkness behind the house.

Tomorrow perhaps, there may be something moving at Whakaipo.

October 5

Something was moving today at Whakaipo all right!

Last night's southerly blast had slackened a little but the waves came smashing into the beach, forcing the stream parallel to the shore and stirring up a turgid soup of rubbish from the bottom. The opaque brown mass, thick with weed and dead leaves, heaved and slopped around my knees as I tried to cast beyond it. The dark stain spread forty or fifty yards out into the lake and it was quite impossible to reach clear water.

26

Stopped off at Acacia Bay Point on the way home. For once the southerly wasn't blowing round corners and I worked a Hamill's Killer deep along the base of the rocks close in. Twice, drawing it out to cast again, a fish made a pass but turned away at the last second. Changed to my favourite Hairy Dog but this brought no response.

At last, right on the bottom, where the weed picked at it now and then, a solid pull drew the fly into a fish. A long and stubborn fight, then as Mount Tauhara vanished behind a veil of rain across the lake, I put the net under a bulky hook-jawed brownie who weighed 6¼lb when I got him home.

Hamill's Killer

October 8

I've tried to interest Bill in fly fishing but he'll have none of it. 'I want a couple of fish to take back to Auckland,' he tells me, 'but spare me all that sodding around with flies. Let's get the boat out and drag a few in.'

And so it was today, a gloomy grey sort of morning with a light easterly blowing a moderate chop from across the lake. In Te Kumi Bay I throttled the motor down to a hesitant idle and handed the six-foot spinning rod to Bill. The green Flatfish dived and wriggled its way across the bay and we headed for Rangatira Rocks.

Bill dropped a newly-lit cigarette as the rod suddenly clattered on the transom and the reel screamed. He yelped as the reel handles rapped his knuckles and held the rod high. I cut the motor and the boat slewed around in the breeze. Bill began to reel in. The fish made another run, lost ground and soon came to the net.

'Not bad, eh?' Bill said as he watched me unhook the fat little fish.

I ran the rule over it and shook my head. 'Sorry — it's just under fourteen inches. Has to go back.'

His face fell but he said nothing as I dropped it over the side. I started the motor again, he flicked the Flatfish into the wake and peeled off line. We watched the rod point nodding rhythmically as the Flatfish dug deeper. As we rounded Rangatira Point the reel screamed again and a good fish lifted out sixty yards behind. This was a better one — there was no question of applying the length test.

We took another two in the deep water close in to Whakamoenga Point and two more backtracking over the same course. Bill was delighted. One of them was more than 5lb, his best yet. He insisted we have one of his fish for lunch. I rolled the fillets from a 3-pounder in seasoned flour and fried them in butter. 'That's the way to get them alright,' Bill enthused. 'How often d'you bring home five fish in one morning doing it your way?'

Sometimes but not often, I told him, but I got greater satisfaction 'doing it my way'.

Bill shrugged. 'Oh well, I suppose one man's meat is another man's poisson.' He laughed immoderately and finished off the last of the trout.

October 12

Haven't been out since Bill was here last week. Not from choice, but of necessity. Interior painting isn't my favourite pastime but it's one of those chores which must be done sooner or later.

Trevor came in for a cup of coffee this morning and I was surprised to learn that he'd known Taupo more than fifty years ago. When he was a child his family lived 140 kilometres south of here at Taihape, where his father ran a sawmill. Almost every holiday was spent at the Tokaanu Hotel at the southern end of the lake.

The State Highway we know today bears little resemblance to the dirt road they used to cover by horse and gig over a period of two days and a night. They were packed in tightly with provisions, camping gear for the night on the road, rifles, fishing tackle and all the other holiday

28

equipment. It was a rare trip he tells me when they failed to shoot a red deer on the Desert Road. This would be loaded onto the already overcrowded gig for the attention of the cook when they reached their destination. Trevor recalls the Desert Road as bleak and formidable in bad weather — as it still is today — but always fascinating, especially to a small boy. And he recalls waking one still and icy dawn to see the first rays of the sun spotlight the blinding white of Ruapehu's crown. The beauty of it brought tears to his eyes, he said, a nine-year-old boy usually too involved with catapults, fishing rods and sweets to be affected by the wonders of nature.

It was the arrival at Tokaanu which set the tone for the holiday. Riding tired but high, they arrived at the village to be cheered in like visiting royalty by the local Maoris.

But it was the fishing that caught my imagination. Trevor told me of one day when three of the family landed forty-two fish, all over 8lb. They kept twelve, the best 17½lb. The mind boggles.

Mostly they trolled with a spoon, although some were caught from the shore with a big lure fly. A dead cockabully, either trolled behind the boat or fished with a fly rod in deep water was good medicine. Things have changed since Trevor's boyhood. Not long after this the massive build-up of fish led to a downturn in the food supply. Size and condition deteriorated. An extensive netting programme removed many tons of trout from the lake, and native smelt from Lake Rotorua were successfully introduced as a forage fish. The programme rehabilitated the fishing but never to the glory of earlier days.

Conditions here have been relatively stable for the past many years and, if the effects of the huge Tongariro power scheme aren't too detrimental, Taupo should remain the most consistent major rainbow trout fishery in the world. But I wish I'd seen it fifty years ago.

October 14

The October easterly drove across the lake at us again today, and our lovely kowhai tree wept golden tears on the lawn. The early lettuce is showing now, tiny bunches clustering in the rows where I sowed the seed too thickly. This morning a pair of tuis came to investigate the red-hot pokers, but they're too early for blossom nectar. And a small flock of silvereyes gave a show-off performance of aerobatics in and out of the birches. They made off smartly when Herman came down from the sundeck to admire them at closer range.

Set up the fly-vice before dinner tonight and tied up half a dozen Hairy Dogs, following old John's pattern of red, yellow or green wool body with an underlay of opossum fur lying back between the strands of wool. A short tail of darkish goat or dog fur completes the dressing. It looks totally undistinguished and many fishermen are rude about its mediocre appearance. But I value the opinion of the trout far more than theirs. Fish continue to take it when much of the sparse dressing has been chewed off, and its main advantage, especially when night fishing, is that the short tail never gets caught up around the bend of the hook.

Kowhai

Tauhou - Silvereye

October 15

A grey morning at the near end of Te Kumi Bay. Two slabby fish, a dark old jack who would have weighed the best part of 7lb before spawning, and a thin colourless hen who came ashore like a wet sack. Both went back to fatten up for the summer. Many fishermen kill these spent fish assuming that they won't recover. But I believe most of them do mend themselves and I like to think that at least they have the chance. Even if they die, the koura will benefit and there's nothing a trout likes better than a good mouthful of freshwater crayfish.

October 21

Back home after four days in Auckland. Can't say I'm sorry although it was good to see various friends there.

The garden has shot away even in that short time. Dark royal blue blooms cover the ceanothus on the lawn, and sweet william glows warm and pink around the back porch. The tomato plants, carefully watered by a neighbour in our absence, are now seven or eight inches tall, ready for planting out in a few days. Baby courgette plants have spread their leaves wide in the seed box and they will go into place soon.

John rang shortly after we got home last night to say that some good fish had been taken at the Hatepe Stream mouth the previous day and what about a trip down there on Sunday? I allowed myself to be persuaded. I must say it's good to be home!

October 24

Skeins of high cirrus stretched across the morning sky when we parked under the poplars at Hatepe. The sun was warm on our faces but it's not summer yet and we pulled oilskin parkas over the chest waders. The rip, stained from yesterday's rain in the hills, curved away to the left from the push of the northerly breeze. Four anglers picket-fenced the rip, knitting in their lines against the current. One came sloshing back through the smooth pool above the bar.

'Landed two before daylight,' he told us. 'But it seems pretty dead now. Think I'll have some breakfast and try them later on.' He clumped away towards one of the baches amongst the trees.

John went in where the inner curve of the dark river water merged with the blue of the lake. He began to cast the Hare and Copper nymph into the rip, letting it swing around into clear water then casting again. I waded in fifty yards further down, pitching the Lord's Killer lure towards the brown water and twitching it back, coiling the floating line in my left hand. There was a shout from John and I looked across to see the rod arched well back over his shoulder and a fish plunging in the curve of the rip. I reeled in and walked back. It was a fine jack, well mended from early spawning. John plucked the nymph from the lower jaw, lifted the fish carefully in both hands and returned it to the water.

'Nicely done,' I said. 'Looks as though the nymph's the thing.' I bit off the lure and tied on a brown caddis nymph.

We took six fish between us during the next two hours, all on the nymph. The best, a lovely 5-pounder, John kept for his smoker. We fished for a further half-hour without a touch then returned to the beach to eat our lunch. We watched the three remaining anglers in the rip, but nothing seemed to be happening.

'I suppose one must give them credit for being free of nymphomania,' John remarked.

Sprawled under the whispering poplars we drank coffee

Lord's Killer

from the thermos and talked idly. A small launch chattered quietly far out beyond the rip and the long grass under the trees nodded to the wind.

We landed another fish apiece after lunch, then the breeze died completely so we took the rods down and started for home. Near the top of the Hatepe Hill I pulled over and stopped the car. We looked back over the valley where the pencil slim poplars marked the winding course of the lower river and the highway bridge showed white against the dark bush. Beyond, at the mouth of the river, the clustered poplars stood tall beside the shining lake.

October 27

Took the Scottie pup fishing for the first time today and perhaps my choice of venue was a poor one.

The rocks at Whakamoenga Point drop almost sheer into deep water. Brodie scuttled around like a large black beetle, poking her long nose into everything at random. Within five minutes she'd fallen into a crevasse. A few minutes after being rescued from the crevasse she fell into a deep cutting and I had to lie full-length to reach her scruff. She seemed delighted and shook herself over my trouser legs.

I told her to sit while I tried to concentrate on the business in hand. The first fish leapt magnificently and the reel shrieked as it drove for the bottom. Immediately Brodie was beside me, yapping hysterically and bouncing stiff-legged with excitement. The fish broached and the barking rose to manic intensity.

Minutes later I steered the beaten fish towards the waiting net. Brodie watched intently, stubby legs braced against the slope of the rock. As I tried to ease the fish over the rim of the net, she fell in on top of it. The hook pulled out and the fish vanished into the depths. She was hauled out again, shook herself over me a second time then ran around in tight circles barking frenetically.

I continued bravely for a further hour and managed to land one decent fish without her assistance. She stayed ashore for this one but later, reaching out to snap at a piece of floating twig, the lake claimed her once more and I was called to the rescue. At this stage I decided to call it a day and we went home.

'How did you get on?' Nick asked as we came in.

'Oh marvellous,' I replied through clenched teeth. 'Marvellous. She fell in three times and lost me a fish.'

Nick laughed gaily. 'Well never mind. She certainly seems to have enjoyed herself — you'll have to take her again.'

I sighed and went to put away my gear.

October 30

A wonderful day — and I didn't even go fishing. The feel of summer is here at last, although we won't have its official blessing for another month.

The day dawned sharp and clear and I could no more stay inside than fly in the air. It was hot enough for me to have my shirt off in the garden and Nick gave her new swimsuit a dry run on the sundeck.

I planted out the tomatoes, also courgette, pumpkin and cucumber seedlings. I'm gambling their lives on no further frosts. Some of the runner beans have just poked above the compost mulch and soon they'll be twining serpentine tendrils around the poles.

Kingfishers are into their breeding season now and while I worked in the garden, one repeated his monotonous 'wheep-whee-wheep' from the telegraph wires along the road. Probably voicing a territorial challenge to rivals but there was no response. Once he stopped long enough to dive-bomb a lizard in the roadside grass. Herman's indignant face rose from the grass a few feet away. He takes his territorial rights seriously too.

Well past eight o'clock now. The town lights across the

water are pricking on one by one and the backdrop of Mount Tauhara lies like a pregnant woman caught in the rosy afterglow. The surface of the lake is black and dense and in the bay below a steady white and a smaller green light creep slowly towards the launch moorings.

On the point a cigarette or a pipe glows briefly. Through the binoculars I can just make out a darker figure against the dark lake.

October 31

Kingfisher still 'wheeping' away when we left for Rotorua this morning. Stopped briefly at Huka Falls and stood on the bridge to feel the monstrous power of the torrent thundering between the compressing rock walls. The wide pool above is an incredible deep blue, smooth and placid until it gathers speed to be sucked into the vortex of the falls. A carefully placed dry fly can sometimes take a fish in this pool. Home again just before dark. The kingfisher was still at it. Don't suppose he's stopped all day.

Kotare - Kingfisher

November

Hatepe Stream

November 1

Another lovely morning. Wide clear blue skies flecked with high cirrus. Took our lunch down to the Waikato above Huka Lodge and lazed on the grass in the sun. We gathered cress to eat with our sandwiches. It was hot and slightly bitter on the tongue.

Had a few casts below the picnic ground. The river is glass-clear, blue and fast — perfect fishing water you would think. And so it was once, when the rich and famous from all over the world came to fish this stretch of river. But that was before the Aratiatia Dam was built and the control gates erected below the outflow from the lake. Now it's sterile by comparison. Fluctuating water levels have ruined the habitat and the natural rhythm of the water-born insects' life cycle and the fishing has suffered accordingly. Trout are still here but there are few of any size and the fishing is inconsistent.

I took a bright 1½-pounder, held it up for Nick to see then returned it to the water. We drove on to the Wairakei Hotel, had a leisurely glass of beer and came home.

37

November 3

Marvellous run of weather over the past three days. Really warm but with a mild southerly to temper the heat of the afternoon.

Seed sowing and planting out are completed for the time being and it's now a matter of judicious watering and tweaking of weeds. The vegetable plot is covered with a thick layer of bush compost. Wonderful stuff and completely free apart from expenditure of a little petrol and a fair bit of energy. The black, sweet-smelling mulch keeps most of the weeds down, attracts worms and deters slugs and snails. But some of the stronger weeds force through and I make a quick daily round if possible.

A native pigeon landed in the pines behind the house just before lunch, the closest to home I've ever seen one. Magnificent birds, like portly aldermen in their striking blue, bronze and white outfits. I sidled over towards the pines to get a closer look but he saw me coming and took off with a clatter of wings, beating strongly up to the native bush higher on the hill. The fat kereru was a favourite dish of the Maoris in other times. They caught him by placing little wooden troughs filled with miro berries in the trees, with strangling snares along the sides of the trough. Today a meal of kereru will cost you $200 — if you're caught. One of my books gives a recipe for cooking them, if one happens to fall dead at your feet as you pass a tree.

After dinner tonight I'm going to Whakaipo with Frank. Not wildly keen on night-fishing, but it does make a complete change and it can be rewarding if conditions are right.

November 4

As black as the inside of your hat. No moon, no stars, a good cloud cover and a bit of a breeze. That's the prescription for night-fishing according to the pundits.

Well last night wasn't like that at all.

Kereru - Native Pigeon

The moon was well up when we arrived at Whakaipo,
sailing full and silver-white above the bluff at the far end of
the bay. The day's light breeze had died and the surface of
the lake was mirror-smooth. The Mapara Stream muttered
softly over the gravel bar, carrying its ripple straight out into
the lake and the wavelets flushed and sighed along the beach.

39

Two anglers were already deep in the rip and we went in well to the left. Neither had touched a fish. Probably too early, they said, and anyway conditions weren't right.

I waded around the fallen tree and began to cast the Hairy Dog across the path of the reflected moon. The air was warm and dense, pressing close like an enveloping garment. Midges whined in my ears and a courting opossum coughed and rattled in the shoreline bush. The small sounds of the night were accentuated by the pervasive silence — the hiss and swish of Frank's line over to my right and the occasional quiet comment passing between the two other men.

Something grabbed the fly briefly and let go. Stripping the line back through the rings I dug for the torch in the waders pouch, turning back inshore to see if the fly was weeded. The hook point was quite clear. Lowering the beam to the water I saw a semi-circle of tiny green-glowing eyes staring up at me from the pumice floor of the lake. Koura were out and about, if nothing else, and it was probably one of these that had grabbed the fly.

It was after ten when we heard the other two wind in and slosh back to the beach. A few minutes later their car started up and they were away. We both moved towards the stream mouth. Suddenly Frank was into a fish. I heard him call out first, then the heavy plunge on the surface. The reel screeched, stopped, screeched again, then I heard the lower notes as he began to regain line. By the time I reached him his torch was on to show a chunky brown flapping on the stones.

We waded out into the rip again and within minutes I hooked a fish, a small rainbow which went back. Just before eleven a silver ripple began to liven the surface of the bay. The new breeze came in fresh and cool, fluttering the leaves of the poplars above the stream mouth. As I wound in something hit the fly with startling force, dragging the rod point down into the water. I felt a heavy throbbing resistance, the reel screamed once, and then the line went slack. When I reeled in again the Hairy Dog had gone.

We scrambled up the bank as the wind strengthened, roaring in the big macrocarpa above the car. Scattered cloud wrack came flying up over the cliffs at the far end of the bay and as we drove up the track from the lake, the rising wind thrashed and fretted the trees against the racing clouds.

November 5

Guy Fawkes' Day, peppered with pops and bangs throughout. Brodie doesn't approve at all and says so repeatedly. Herman retired under the house when the spasmodic barrage began to build up shortly after dark. We've been watching from the sundeck, counting more than twenty bonfires glowing in and around the town across the lake. Rockets curve up into the night sky, bursting in sprays of falling stars which are quickly blotted out against the blackness. Late now, and the sputtering blasts continue, punctuated by Brodie's weakening response.

November 6

Mostly in the garden, picking up the odd dead rocket, weeding and earthing up the potatoes. They've just appeared above the mulch, tender green leaves reaching for the sun. Also repaired a hole Brodie has dug in the vegetable patch. I trench with garden and kitchen refuse, including trout heads and tails. Usually they're buried deep enough but her long nose found a couple of ripe heads and she sat happily chewing them on the lawn this morning. They impart a certain aura so she's not allowed in the house for two days at least.

Roast wild pork for dinner tonight.

November 8

Frank rang this afternoon to suggest another evening at Whakaipo. I said thanks but no, I had work to do. This wasn't strictly true. I enjoy night-fishing sometimes but not too often. For me, the visual rewards of fishing in the dark are strictly limited.

So I finished what I had to do, cleaned the car, then helped Nick prepare dinner. Last night we roasted a leg of the young boar I shot in the 10/80 forest some weeks ago. Wonderful stuff, rich and gamy as bland domestic pork never is. Tonight it cut firm and still moist, beautifully complemented by Don's early buttercrunch lettuce and French Breakfast radishes straight out of the garden.

42

Ruru - Morepork

A walk with the dog up into Mapara Road after dinner.
Another lovely evening. In the fading light we sat for a
while on the roadside bank looking out over the lake
towards the town. Mount Tauhara stood black against the
reflected glow of the dying sun. How short-lived the sunsets
are. You'd think something so magnificent would last for a
long time but it doesn't. The colours change almost as you
watch. Within minutes the crimson cools into orange, then
yellow, until at last the pale cold green holds for moments
only and then all the colour is gone. The hills fold into the
darkness and the shivering stars begin to prick through one
by one.

As we walked slowly back in the warm dark, a morepork
owl complained from the pines on the hillside.

November 10

This is an unsolicited testimonial:
Specification: Length, 7ft in two pieces. Weight, 5ozs. Material, split bamboo cane. Cork handle with Duralumin moveable reel fittings and screw-in rubber button. Agate-lined rings throughout. Model, "Midget" trout spinning rod. Maker, Farlow of Haymarket, London.

I was thirteen or fourteen when I bought it — or my parents did. It cost thirty-five shillings. My "Midget" has played many roles over the years. In England it has caught roach, rudd, perch, bream, tench, dace, carp, chub and eels. I've used it to spin for pike and trout in England, for trout in Ireland, Scotland, mainland Australia, Tasmania and New Zealand. It's landed three salmon up to 12lb in Ireland and numerous hard-fighting kahawai in New Zealand. It's worn centre-pin reels, threadline reels and multipliers. I've had it with me always for more than forty years. But nothing lasts for ever.

Today, with young David from the Lodge, I was throwing a small spoon off Whakamoenga Rocks. One cast went awry and there was a queer cracking sound. I reeled in, cast again, there was another cracking sound and the rod sagged in the middle. The "Midget" had split its top section just above the ferrule. The cane had rotted from the inside and the strips had fallen apart.

I'd like to write to Messrs Farlow, not to complain about their product, but to commend them for making a rod that has served so long and efficiently. But I discover that Farlows is no more, swallowed up by some larger organisation and now consigned to anonymity. This is as sad as having broken the rod. I still recall my visit as an eight- or nine-year-old to that magic emporium in the Haymarket where, with a birthday ten-shilling note clutched in a hot hand, I marvelled at the Aladdin's Cave of treasures displayed there.

The rod can be repaired but Farlows can't be brought back.

November 11

Rain most of the day, not hard but persistent. Yesterday's
brassy heat broke with a thunderstorm in the late afternoon.
You could almost smell it coming — hot and still with a
strange pressure in the ears. Then bruised purple clouds
building up in the south and the ominous rumble coming
louder and closer each time. It was a relief when the rain
came at last. It's been coming down ever since but I don't
think it'll last.

November 12

Wrong again, still raining! But it's doing the garden a power
of good.

Nick and I sorted through some old photos this evening
and came across one of my father as a young man. Very like
me, Nick says, but better-looking. The old fellow was no
fisherman unfortunately so there was little practical
encouragement for me from home. On one of the only two
occasions I took him fishing, he impaled his thumb with a
large sea-fishing hook and we had to find a doctor to remove
it. The other time saw him manfully but with small
enthusiasm row me around Lake Windermere in the English

lake district in a vain attempt at trolling for pike. Perhaps if he'd been a fisherman he might have lived longer. But his only real interest outside the home was business and that's probably what killed him too soon.

I always had the impression he thought his last-born a little dim to be obsessed with so inconsequential and flippant an occupation as fishing.

November 14

A letter with a strange and colourful stamp arrived today. All the way from Guam, it told us that Gene would spend a couple of days with us on his way home for Christmas with his parents in Arkansas.

This is fine with us. Gene works for an American airline and enjoys the advantages of heavily discounted travel. Much of his vacation time is spent trout fishing. He's been to Taupo twice before, once with a colleague when I took them trolling and fly fishing, and again with his parents last year. They stayed at a local motel and on their second day, while Gene and myself flogged the water to foam with fly gear, the old folks went trolling in a charter launch. We caught two small rainbows between us and the trollers, who had never fished for trout before, came back with eight good fish, the best a 7½-pounder caught by Gene's mother. A few caustic remarks were passed over drinks that night. We look forward to Gene's arrival. We'll be trying to cap his mother's performance.

November 15

Nick decided Brodie would benefit from a few hours at Te Kumi Bay with me today.

Dogs can make good fishing companions. Some dogs, that is, not ours. But what she lacks in pleasant companionship is amply compensated for by hysterical enthusiasm.

Wading the shallow margins of Te Kumi Bay doesn't offer scope for falling in from great heights such as Whakamoenga Rocks provide, but she spent all her time in the water all the same. I encouraged her — if that's the right word — to stay close to shore rather than tread water beside me or continually circumnavigate my position. A glance over the shoulder every so often revealed a poignant, spindly-legged object either crouching on a rock or standing chest-deep and gazing anxiously in my direction.

I hooked a fish and immediately the usual hysterical outburst ensued. She began to steam strongly out towards the scene of battle and tried to grab the fish when it came close. Eventually I managed to beach it without her help. Later, during a brief spell on dry land, her busy nose found a wasps' nest. The outcry brought me stumbling from the water in great haste. Flailing wildly at the angry wasps, I managed to pick her up and hurl her into the lake, then cantered off along the beach beating off the pursuing insects until they gave up the chase — but not before stinging me twice on the back of one hand. The dog had the sense to stay in the water until the wasps had dispersed, then she paddled slowly down the shore to where I sat sucking my hand.

Nick is sympathetic, but pleased that Brodie enjoyed her outing. My stings are still painful. The dog's, if in fact she has any, don't seem to worry her at all.

Brown Trout

November 20

Home again after three days with Ken and Meg at Rotorua. Ken showed us a lovely 9¾lb brownie that he'd taken on the evening before we arrived. He'd hooked it under the big willow where the Ngongotaha River joins the lake within thirty yards of the house. It hung cold and firm and beautiful in the larder, leopard-spotted and tawny-gold, freckled with points of scarlet. The flesh in the gut cavity was deep orange. We had cutlets of it deep-fried that night, served with a sharp tartare sauce and cos lettuce from the garden.

Ken doesn't fish after dark very often. The weight of years, poor eyesight and other infirmities make it difficult for him. So I took his rod down to the river after dinner and in the darkness under the trees worked a little deer hair lure of Ken's making up against the flow of the stream. Twice I hooked something very heavy, but for moments only. The second time after an almost imperceptible take, the rod tip pulled down with a savage jolt, the reel's stutter rose to a scream, and the fly let go, or so I thought. Reeling in I found it had gone, the leader broken cleanly at the knot.

Ken has taken brownies up to 12½lb here.

November 23

Roy likes to fish the Waikato River for an hour or so after work, and this evening we went in close to the piggery off Spa Road, where a hot thermal stream joins the river. The stream heats the piggery in winter, which must make it one of the few in the world with this natural advantage.

I fished a dry Cochybondhu upstream although there was no visible rise and Roy worked a Red Setter lure on a sinking line below the outlet of the stream. I landed and released two medium rainbow, then when it was too dark to see the fly on the water, came back downstream to Roy. His dark figure was waist deep in the river, the rod arched against the waning afterglow.

Cochybondhu

Rainbow Trout

'I've had it on for about ten minutes,' he told me. 'It's a good one but I think I've got it coming now.'

The fish boiled on the dark surface close in and I sidled around to try and get behind. It saw me and drove out into the strong middle water, stealing fifteen yards of hard-won line. Roy held it firmly, wound the rod tip down to the water and lifted. The fish grudgingly gave ground and came closer. Now it was within feet of the bank and I managed to get behind as it floundered in the shallows. It turned flank up and Roy stepped back carefully, walking it within the arch of the rod. I put the side of my boot behind it and hefted it ashore.

At Roy's house we toasted the nickel-bright 7½lb rainbow in the best Scotch whisky. It's the heaviest fish either of us have ever taken from the Waikato.

November 25

John says he's heard the smelt are starting to move in the Western Bays. Good news. To me, smelting is the most exciting fishing Taupo can offer. The swarming millions of tiny glass-clear galaxia minnows are an important source of food for trout ravaged by spawning. These, and the later green manuka beetle, are the major factors in the recovery of spawned fish. Massive clouds of smelt begin to move close inshore at this time of year to spawn and feed on minute chironomid flies. And it's here that the trout are waiting for them with savage appetite.

Whanganui Bay would be a good starting point, John suggests, so we've made a date for next week. Barrett's bach at Waihi, down at the southern end of the lake, will be our base for two days.

Now I must set up the vice to tie half a dozen Hawk and Rabbit smelt flies against the day.

November 30

Milling thousands of people, the roar of traffic and the capital's ubiquitous winds funnelling between the concrete canyons of the inner city. The scenario of the past three days has left me stimulated perhaps, but also sincerely grateful that I don't live there any more. The urban pace, moderate by overseas standards, is something I can do without.

Few cities in the world have Wellington's natural advantages of location. The high amphitheatre of the central city embraces a harbour of surpassing beauty. The lookout from Mount Victoria on a fine day, offers a panorama unmatched almost anywhere in the world. From the topmost cable-car terminal the more concentrated picture of the harbour is a beautifully balanced work of art, and from the top of Wright's Hill, 600 metres above sea level, the view can take your breath away.

And now I'm home. The 400-kilometre drive is tiring and I'm glad it's over. But the trip was worthwhile in more ways than one, not least the warm satisfaction of returning to Taupo.

December

Whakamoenga Rocks

December 1

A quiet poke around the garden today. There's change and progress even after four days. Second sowing of radishes almost ready and Nick has used the first of the buttercrunch lettuce. Runner beans are twined lovingly halfway up the poles and second crop broad beans six or seven inches high.

Our resident song thrush tossed off an aria from the big silver birch this morning. Found him a snail from the rockery and threw it on the lawn. When I walked away he flew down to pick it up and then over to the road to crack it. Herman's enigmatic yellow gaze followed the whole operation closely, but the warmth and comfort of the sundeck chair ruled out any active involvement.

December 4

Blue Damsel Fly

The Whanganui Stream is born in scree and wind-burned tussock high up in the foothills south-west of Lake Taupo. It winds a stony course through steep grazing country before bringing its tribute to the lake by way of a deep and narrow gorge. Access from the highway to the mouth is more like a mountain-goat track than a road and calls for careful driving and steady nerves.

Yesterday morning we had the place to ourselves. The river poured smoothly over the bar, bearing towards the right-hand side of the bay, where a white-faced heron lifted away from the shallows as we scrunched across the pumice strand. On the far side of the rip a deputation of red-billed gulls strutted the beach. An early breeze feathered the surface of the lake and the overcast of high light cloud filtered the sun's rays.

A sudden splash churned the stream mouth — three rises one after the other — scattering a quicksilver sprinkle of smelt on the surface. I made first contact, covering a thrashing rise in the same place. A slabby hen went back again as John began to cast towards the inner curve of the rips. He was soon fast to a fish which took him well into the bay before he beached it close to the mouth. Rises were frequent now as the fish harried the smelt in and around the outflow. I watched for a broaching fish, gauged its line of travel and pitched the Hawk and Rabbit in its path to make a fast retrieve. The moving line stopped, the rod came up in a jolting arc and the fish leapt in a glistening parabola.

By eleven o'clock we'd landed twelve fish between us. A few were slabby still, but the bounty of the smelt would soon build them up. We ate our lunch slouched on the warm pumice close to the rip. A few spasmodic rises broke the surface far out, but the only movement near at hand was the quiet chuckle of the outflow. The heron came back, stalking the margins of the rip with exaggerated care. Lifting his feet high out of the water he peered and probed, snaking his head down every now and again to snap up an errant smelt.

52

I noticed a quiet rise just below the mouth, then another. A gentle dimpling of the surface, certainly not a smelt rise. I got up and went closer. 'They're taking bees,' I called back to John. The nearest thing in my fly box was a Ewe Wasp. This was quickly tied on and floated over the rising fish. The subterfuge was acceptable. I hooked and landed two fish, one a slab and the other a respectable 3½-pounder. Then the source of the bees dried up and there were no more rises.

Later in the afternoon we each took a fish on lures swum deep in the rip, then there was a blank patch for an hour or more. At six o'clock there was a brief flurry of smelting and we took three fish. Then we decided to call it a day. We'd landed nineteen between us, the best a little over 6lb, and we were more than satisfied.

This morning we set off from the Waihi bach, eager to be in amongst them again. The day was promising and we hoped to better yesterday's score. But there was no real smelt rise at all and we landed only one fish each. As we drove back to Taupo John was moved to religious philosophising: 'The Lord giveth,' he intoned piously, 'and He also withholdeth when you least expect it.'

Ewe Wasp

December 6

Flashed up the smoker today for the Whanganui fish. Salted and sugared them the same night and they were hung up to dry yesterday. They're doing nicely right now and considering the direction of the breeze, I predict that George will pay a social call sometime tomorrow — just to see how we are.

December 7

Took the .22 along the road to Whakamoenga Rocks early this morning and parked the car at Te Kumi Bay. Walking quietly along the soft pumice margins under the overhang of broom and manuka I often see rabbits along here. And sometimes they sit for me.

A skittery family of Californian quail criss-crossed the road in front, anxious but unwilling to take flight until the last moment. They moved ahead pit-pit-pitting until the cock bird gave his hoarse gathering call, then they whirred up and planed away into the roadside scrub. Two rabbits sat in the middle of the road around the next bend. They saw me but didn't move. Slowly sinking to one knee I lined up the 'scope's cross-hairs on the nearest one's shoulder and squeezed the trigger. It leapt into the air, kicked strongly with its back feet and lay still on the dusty road. The other one paused just long enough for me to get the sights on it and then vanished into the scrub.

Picked up the dead rabbit and walked back to the car. Nick will be pleased, I thought. She loves rabbit and makes a splendid job of stew or pie and also an excellent paté. Herman would be pleased too — a rabbit's foot keeps him amused for hours.

George called in this afternoon — just to see how we were — and was surprised and delighted to learn that there were fish in the smoker. We persuaded him to accept one when they're done.

December 9

Heard today that the smelt are starting to move in at this end of the lake now. Perhaps I'll see if there's anything happening at Whakamoenga tomorrow.

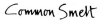

Common Smelt

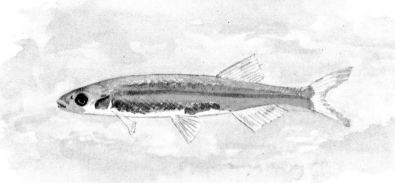

December 10

The high shoulder of volcanic rock affords an almost aquarium-like view into the tiny bay close to the end of the point.

The sun warmed my back as I lay peering through the glass-smooth surface deep down to where the layered plates of rock merge with the bed of the lake. Miniscule diatoms floated in the shafts of sunlight, and cockabullies — black, dappled and fawn — nibbled the patina of algae on the steep rock face. A fish, too far down for me to judge its size, cruised briefly across the floor of the bay and disappeared into deeper water. I shifted uncomfortably as the rock pressed into my knees.

And now I saw them! A wide grey ribbon slowly moving around the slanting buttress of rock, moulding its amorphous form to the contour. Thousands of tiny fish, sparkling like needles where the sun struck through them, came winding a hesitant course into the little bay.

The trout saw them too. One fish darted in from nowhere, cutting a murderous swathe through the shining horde. The shoal scattered in panic and reformed quickly. Another rainbow, white mouth agape, smashed into them from below. The ribbon of smelt broke again and two more trout moved in, hounding them to the surface and against the rock face in an orgy of slaughter. Working like dogs with sheep, they circled the milling smelt, herded them into close concentration then drove through them again and again. Within moments the activity moved away. A flurry of rises churned the surface off the point and they were gone, leaving only a few battered smelt lying on the quiet water.

I picked up the rod and started for the car. There was no breath of wind and chances for a fish were nil. But at least I know the smelt have arrived at this end of the lake.

December 12

Bought a passion fruit plant today, about eighteen inches tall. We tried one before but planted it too late and it didn't survive the winter. Now this one's in a sun-trap position below the deck, guarded on both sides by pieces of rigid plastic. A good summer start should build it up to stand the winter.

Nick loves passion fruit. I'm not quite so keen but I do fancy the exotic image of myself lying in the sun, languidly plucking semi-tropical fruit from a shiny green vine.

December 13

Gene arrives on Thursday and we've been preparing the spare room for him. Just hope the bed's long enough. (Being six-foot-five must present certain problems in this area.) He hasn't been here before when the smelt are running and I hope the conditions are right.

December 15

Shot a hare and two rabbits in a dawn attack up on the hill this morning. Lying under the butter-gold broom flowers, I picked them all off within seconds before they came to their senses. The second rabbit I took with a running shot which was very good for my ego, even if it was more through luck than judgement.

Left them briefly on the sundeck when I got home and looked out moments later to see Herman manhandling the hare over the edge. It's as big as he is but he tipped it over the edge and managed to drag it lion-fashion between his front legs and under the house before I could stop him. Managed to retrieve it after fifteen minutes' hot and dirty work. Herman wasn't pleased and obviously thought me most unreasonable.

Red Admiral

December 16

Gene has grown no smaller. He brought us two bottles of German hock, one of which we had tonight with dinner — dry, cool and astringent, a beautiful complement to our favourite trout recipe. It's *filets de poisson gratinés* from the French cookbook I gave Nick for Christmas last year. The pink fillets are cut into two-inch pieces, placed in a buttered oven dish, seasoned, then covered with chopped mushrooms and onions sautéed in white wine. Breadcrumbs and knobs of butter cover the whole thing and it's cooked in the oven until the crumbs are brown.

Having forgotten Gene's appetite — for this sort of thing anyway — we didn't have enough, so we finished off with rabbit paté on French bread. A reversal of courses but no-one seemed to care.

Gene was in Alaska earlier this year and we heard mind-boggling tales of steelhead and huge tyee salmon taken from rough wilderness camps accessible only by light aircraft.

We had another duty-free Scotch and now Gene's turned in for the night. It's been a long day for him and he wants a clear head for business tomorrow.

December 17

And business was good. Fishing Whakamoenga Point into a stiffish southerly, we hooked nine between us, landed six and brought home two. The sun was bright on the water and our faces tonight are red and stiff. Gene is ecstatic. Smelting is just out of this world, he says, and why hasn't he been here at the right time before?

It took him a short while to get the hang of it but there's nothing hard really if you can punch a cast a short way into the wind. The fish crowd the smelt in close when there's an inshore breeze and this compensates for having to cast against it. He lost three fish, and the flies, probably by striking too hard. When these rainbows are hounding smelt they're moving fast and a mere lifting of the rod point usually hooks them.

Like most good American anglers, Gene rarely kills a fish unless he particularly wants one for the table. But the best of his two, a stocky deep-chested 5½-pounder, came home with us. Three of the six were still in poor shape from spawning but the smelt should soon alter that.

We lowered the level in the Scotch bottle and had a foreleg of wild pork for dinner. New potatoes from the garden, shining dark green silver beet and the first of the baby courgettes. And we had the second bottle of German hock. I doubt if this is the type of wine recommended for game meat, but it didn't seem to matter at all and we enjoyed it enormously.

Whakaipo Bay

December 18

Most of Whakaipo Bay was blanketed with smoky mist at
six this morning. Gene stood back from the stream mouth
and on his first cast hooked a good fish right in the throat of
the rip. It took all his casting line and half the backing in one
run. Then it leapt way out and threw the fly.

We waded quietly around to my favourite little bay and by
this time an early breeze quickened from the south to sweep
away the banks of mist. Smelting fish broached here and
there and we landed three before the breeze died and the sun
polished the smooth surface. All of them went back and we
sat on the rocky beach for a while drinking coffee from the
thermos. Gene talked about the unchanging tropical heat of
Guam and the thick, dense nights when it was hard to sleep,
sweating under the mosquito netting. He'd thought about
Taupo on these nights, he said, and the strong cold rivers of
Alaska that he'd fished earlier this year. 'I guess I'm pretty
lucky really,' he said, 'when I can have spells like this in
between times.'

Wading back to the stream mouth we saw a shining
cuckoo dipping between the cool green willows, and a dozen
or so mallard cruising and dabbling a cautious distance from
the shore.

We took Brodie to Rangatira Rocks this afternoon but
came back fishless. Flat calm, still blue water and no
smelting rise. We fished deep with sinking lines but there
was nothing down there either.

Miles away to the south, Ruapehu reared slate grey against
the hot sky, a shawl of white draped over its peak. Beside it,
Ngauruhoe's cone trailed a thin plume of dark smoke.

Tonight, Gene's last, we spent two hours at the Tupara
Road groin, casting towards the lights pricking the darkness
on the far side of the lake. I landed a gaunt, hook-jawed
brownie who should have weighed 10 or 11lb, and two
small rainbow. Gene, fishing a deer hair fly which looked
suspiciously like a small mouse, took a lovely fat

4½-pounder which I would have kept for the freezer. But he eased it back into the water with the expressed hope that they'd meet again the next time he was in Taupo.

We had a late supper and a couple of drinks with Nick. Gene leaves tomorrow for Auckland and flies to Los Angeles the following night. He'll be home with the family the day before Christmas Eve.

December 20

Nick's family due up from Wellington for Christmas in three days' time. They all enjoyed a leg of venison last time here, so I've got a permit for the 10/80 forest tomorrow to see what I can do. It'll be an early start so bed's the place right now.

December 21

Moths still flickered in the headlights as the car lurched over the tussock track. I parked well back from the dark hole where the track leads into the native forest, locked the car and clipped a full magazine into the 30.06. A pale saffron glow lifted in the east but inside the cool tunnel of beech and kanuka the darkness pressed close and I trod carefully.

Half a mile in, grey light came filtering through the high canopy, outlining the grey boles of trees on either side. I cut a blaze on a lone rimu for a marker and stepped with exaggerated care onto the narrow side path of dead leaves and rotted twigs. There was no sound and cold drops of moisture dropped onto my face. The air was still and dank and smelt of peat. Now the narrow path straightened to run parallel with the main track and dipped into a narrow gully. A fantail wheeled and fluttered around my head, and in the gaining light a flicker of movement froze me to a halt.

Two red hinds were feeding beyond a fallen beech some fifty yards ahead. One looked up and around briefly, ears

60

twitching before continuing to feed. I sank down in slow
motion until the fallen tree hid me, then moved up quickly
behind it. I rested the rifle on a root, took a deep breath and
centred the cross-hairs on the nearer one's head as she looked
up again.

The shattering report in the close confines of the trees was
deafening. I swiftly bolted another round into the breech,
but there was no need. The fallen hind's back legs kicked
rhythmically and the other beast had vanished. The 30.06
soft-tip had smashed the top half of the head right away.
I dragged the carcass through the loose under-storey and left
it in the middle of the main track. Then I started back to
the car.

Dull gold shafts of sunlight angled through the tall
galleries of beech as I drew up close to the dead hind, and
already the flies had begun to gather. I honed the knife blade
on the stone, paunched the carcass and removed the liver and
back steaks. Then with the small cleaver I chopped through
the spine to release the hindquarters and took off both
forelegs, leaving the thorax, neck and head for the
scavengers. Nick was surprised to see me home by ten
o'clock. I'm still a bit surprised myself. It's not often as easy
as that.

Now, one hindquarter is hanging in the meat safe and the
rest of the beast is wrapped and labelled in the deep-freeze.

December 24

The family is all here now. Nick, with her mother, father
and sister, are concluding a loud and thoroughly dishonest
game of Scrabble. Young Patrick has taken my Hardy
Knockabout down to the Acacia Bay Point and should be
back before now. His choice always falls on the Knockabout

when offered the pick of my armoury, and his casual borrowing of this venerable and distinguished rod would make some pundits froth at the mouth. Reminds me of the choleric retired soldier I met in a Hampshire hotel many years ago. He was railing on about young people in general and his new son-in-law in particular. He'd offered the young man the chance of a day on his expensively rented stretch of the famous River Test. The offer was accepted graciously enough, but he blew the whole thing when he casually asked if he could borrow the old fellow's rod. 'Lend you my rod?' barked the reluctant father-in-law. 'By God, I'd rather lend you my bloody toothbrush!'

Luckily I have no such inhibitions as far as my brother-in-law is concerned.

Tonight Nick excelled herself with the deer liver. She'd sliced and marinated it in sherry beforehand, then made a stroganoff with onions, butter, paprika and sour cream. Served on a bed of fluffy rice it was marvellous. The true identity of the liver was disclosed after the meal much to the horror of her mother. She'd enjoyed it as much as anyone but wouldn't have touched it if she'd known beforehand.

One of the wall lights is focussed on the Christmas tree in the corner, its sparkling tinsel and shining baubles seeming to generate light of their own, and under the tree the brightly wrapped parcels are safe for only a few hours more.

December 25

We all ate and drank too much today and all seem to be very happy with the situation. A noble tom turkey provided the central feature at dinner and apart from the ham, almost everything else came out of the garden including redcurrants as a garnish for the trifle. Patrick came back very late last night but the Knockabout had won him a beautiful 4-pounder from the point. This preceded the main course, boiled and eaten cold with mayonnaise.

62

The presents were a great success — especially my new double tapered air-cell floating line.

December 26

Boxing Day, with unexpected rain lasting almost all day. Not a great deal of constructive activity, although Patrick, fired by previous success, spent a wet hour or so at the point. He caught nothing but his casting certainly seems to be improved.

The rest of us sat around picking at the numerous leftovers, talking and playing Scrabble. We even braved the rain during a brisk walk down to the lodge in the bay for milk and butter.

The rain has stopped now and it's very hot. The weather report tells us that the rude interruption should have passed over by morning and we hope for further sunshine.

December 27

The forecasters were right. Clear and bright all day with a brassy sun alone in the hot blue sky. Dozens of cars and seemingly hundreds of people down at Acacia Bay, the water dotted with boats and swimmers. Further out, water-skiers creamed the smooth surface in wide intersecting arcs.

Took father-in-law to Whakamoenga but the numbers game defeated us. On the eastern face of the rocks two shapely girls in bikinis made tree-felling motions with spinning rods on the left-hand point and on the other, two youths, giving more attention to the bikinis than their fishing, were casting lures on deep-sinking lines. Despite the indiscriminate hail of metal on the left point, trout rose spasmodically to the darting smelt. The two youths observed similar activity at their location, but made no attempt to raise their sights to the scene of action. Very frustrating, but I'm not presumptuous enough to tell others how they should fish. I took Nigel to the southern side but here what looked like a swimming carnival was in progress, and the sinister black forms of snorkel divers paddled face down across the surface. So we went home and sat on the deck with a flagon of cool beer.

Later we watched the sun set in a dramatic conflagration of fiery red. It faded quickly to glowing orange and eventually the soft enveloping darkness obliterated pregnant Tauhara across the lake.

December 30

The family returned to Wellington today. New Year's Eve commitments have to be met and both Nigel and Patrick return to work within the week. Very quiet around the house and we miss them. Even Brodie and Herman seem strangely subdued after all the lavish attention. Hot and bright and the lake still traced by ski-towing launches and the slower trolling craft. Can't say I'll be sorry when the holidays are over.

December 31

Spent most of the afternoon in the garden, tying up the green peas and bracing the broad beans on either side with baling twine. Culled some of the sprouting tops for tonight's dinner with ham and the remains of the venison. Tonight we see in the New Year with friends in town. Just hope it's not too hot and crowded.

January

Kuratau River Mouth

January 1

Cooler today, mercifully, and we didn't get up until after ten. My mouth was a bit arid until well into the afternoon. Nick is in better shape but likewise a little frayed around the edges. We swore we'd leave as soon as midnight traditions had been observed but it was after two when we got home. Spent a very quiet day and this evening walked the dog up Mapara Road. It's still quite early but I think we'll soon be in bed. I'll stretch my new floating line between the trees tonight and take it down before the morning sun gets to it.

January 4

I don't often go to Kuratau. It's about eighty kilometres from home, way down at the south-western end of the lake and expensive in terms of petrol. Never actually fished the dam itself — too many tackle-grabbing dead trees for my taste — but have done quite well at the river mouth and the

Sandspit close by. Nick's spending a couple of days in Rotorua with Ken and Meg so she wasn't going to be sitting at home pining for me.

Hawk and Rabbit

Hadn't really expected the strong northerly piling surf into the beach. Half a dozen anglers already there at ten in the morning and sensibly concentrating on the river mouth and the sheltered side of the Sandspit. Fishing with the crowd is not for me, so I came back to the north-facing beach where the pouncing waves stirred up a brown soup of pumice silt and weedy rubbish. The mess cleared about thirty feet out and fish were slashing at smelt in the clear water. Before I had the Hawk and Rabbit punched into the teeth of the wind, a cunning breaker sidled up and slapped me in the face leaving a gallon or so down the front of the chest waders. Back-pedalled and tried again. Rising on tiptoe to avoid the next assault, I managed to pitch the fly beyond the dirty water and started a fast retrieve. The rod point dipped at once and a good fish arched into the air. Five minutes later a handsome 4-pounder thrashed up onto the sand. It was packed to the gills with smelt. I hastily buried it and returned to the fray.

Within an hour, I landed six more fish and hooked and lost four others. The smallest 3lb and the best just over 5lb. I was sodden. Water dripped from the end of my nose as I gutted the seven fish and humped them back to the river mouth and the car. Carried the spoils with head modestly bowed past my fellow fishers and stowed them in the boot. Drove home with my wet backside on an old towel, but I didn't care. A well-nourished ego compensates for many discomforts.

January 6

Herman and Brodie turned on a wonderful performance for Nick's return last night. Battle surged back and forth across the polished boards of the lounge, Herman repeatedly counter-attacking against the Scottie's long-nosed assault.

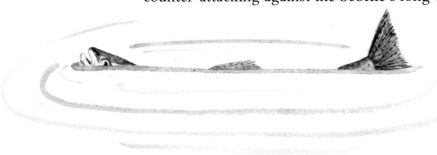

The cat has the best of the issue most of the time. Brodie's weight and low centre of gravity send her spinning and scrabbling on the smooth floor, galloping furiously on the spot to get nowhere at all. Herman follows up with lightning lefts and rights but is invariably conned into close combat and gets mumbled wetly in the long jaws leaving his splendid coat damp and patchy. He also leaves small grey pieces of it lying around in the aftermath of battle.

Picked up two or three cast-off strands this morning and tied them along a No. 8 hook, first dressed with a creamy rabbit body. This afternoon at Te Kumi Bay the Cat and Rabbit smelt took two good fish.

Tonight both protagonists are sleeping peacefully on the mat by the French window. Must say Brodie's wiry pelt looks quite attractive in the dying light of the sun. Perhaps I should tie up some Black Hairy Dogs for my next night-fishing sortie?

Green Manuka Beetle

January 7

Suddenly, the green manuka beetle are up and about. They're late this year. Usually they appear around Christmas which may or may not account for their scientific name of *Pyronota festiva*. Frankly I doubt it, but it's a nice thought.

Took our lunch to Whakamoenga Rocks today and there were undulating rafts of them slopping thickly in the cuttings and inlets. Others bumbled about in the air, entangling themselves in Nick's hair and hooking their chestnut legs lightly in our clothing. They hatch out amongst the roots of the manuka and during their brief span, provide the trout with a valuable build-up after spawning.

Today was hot and windless and I didn't bother putting up the rod. Occasionally a fish delicately sipped a beetle from the surface. Fantails and the odd warbler hawked them around the trees back from the water. Early this evening in the fresh ripple at Whakaipo, I tried for an hour, first with

Green Beetle Fly

green beetle replica, then a dry Cochybondhu. Fish were taking the natural here and there but there were far too many of them for my offering to be seriously considered.

January 9

Smoked trout for breakfast today, simmered in milk for me, *au naturel* with lemon juice and black pepper for Nick.

Weeded around the sweet corn while Nick did her stint at the radio station. Corn's looking really good — strong, tall and green. Soon the pale gold tops will be breaking out. No signs of cobs yet but they always fool me like this before coming away with a rush. Picked up Nick from her broadcasting and we had a long glass of beer at the Lake Hotel. Thought I might do more in the garden after lunch but luckily it came on to rain, so I tried the new sofa for size, well backed up by cushions.

Seems to be satisfactory — Nick woke me two hours later with a cup of tea.

January 11

Mostly writing the last couple of days. Weather brassy hot and useless for fishing. A few hopeful holiday trollers about but they're outnumbered by the fizz-boats and their water-ski attachments.

Took a break this afternoon while Nick was out shopping and lay down on the sofa listening to Mozart's Piano Concerto No. 1 in stereo. Had it turned well up and the incredibly moving pulse beat filled the house with sound.

What a man! Dead by his mid-thirties but forever alive. Got up to turn the record and looked out into the garden. A small hedgehog crouched in the middle of the lawn. Had he been attracted by the music? I don't know but I went down to speak to him and he was quite unafraid, blinking short-sightedly in the unaccustomed sunshine. I brought him a slice of bread dampened with milk and he ate it greedily from my hand. Nick came home as he was finishing it off and he was quite unworried by her too. Completed his unexpected snack and shambled off into the bushes on spindly brown legs.

You rarely see them in broad daylight, so it must have been the Mozart.

January 12

Banked up folds of cloud rode up from the south today but passed over without dropping their burden. The colours of summer often stand out more brightly without the sun. The hills to our right are butter-gold with broom and gorse and behind the house the flowering manuka is iced with small white blossoms.

Picked a basketful of runner beans this afternoon. They're embarrassingly prolific and have to be culled almost daily to stop them growing large and tough. Took some down to George together with one of the Kuratau smoked fish.

January 15

Tried for a rabbit early this morning along the road to Whakamoenga, but saw only one and it was too quick for me. A family of Californian quail panicked across the road in front of me on the way back to the car. Mum and Dad plus eight little balls of fluff, creamy brown spotted with black, completely round and no bigger than a penny.

The garden's looking really lush. A year ago it would have been different, before the water was reticulated from the new reservoir on the hill behind. We had two galvanised rainwater tanks then and supplies had to be carefully conserved in the summer. Our five-fingers have berries for the first time, black tarry clusters bunched among the cool evergreen leaves.

January 17

I'm not a great one for trailing hardware — or flies — behind
a boat. But it's good to get out on the water sometimes, so
we accepted George's offer of a sortie to the Western Bays.

Still and hot as it has been for days now, and the powerful
motor pushed the seventeen-foot hull fast and easily across
the sun-bright surface. In less than half an hour George
throttled down as we approached Cherry Bay, and the two
trolling rods angled out over the transom. There was no
breeze and the miasma of exhaust smoke rode along with us.
It was very hot.

Nick crouched in the half-cabin and I soaked my towelling
hat over the side before putting it on. George was quite
happy under his wide brimmed straw hat, steering with one
hand on the tiller and the other on his rod. Occasional fish
broached the polished surface but nothing took the lures.
After a fishless hour and a half we nosed into Cherry Bay for
lunch. It was cool and dim close to the shore, overhung with
tall native bush. Sun stippled the water through the high
canopy and we saw the odd fish ranging fast across sand
patches between the weed. We ate lettuce and tomato
sandwiches and nursed a can of cold beer apiece.

The chattering chorus of cicadas lulled me into a doze after
a while and when I came to there seemed to be a change in
the atmosphere. We lifted the pick and chugged out into the
lake. The air was still and dense; purple thunderheads spread
from the north-west and we heard the first ominous rumble
repeated and echoed from the high scarps behind us. George
revved the motor, the prow lifted from the water and we set
a fast course for home.

Bruised thunderclouds covered half the sky as the boat's
stem sliced and peeled back the calm surface. A shattering
thunderclap split and crashed above us and rain began to hiss
on the water. Nick sheltered under the fo'c'sle and I covered
myself with the boat's storm canvas. George sat bravely in
the stern, hat pulled down, oilskin buttoned to the chin with

an upside-down pipe clenched between his teeth. The rain boiled on the lake and I imagined I could hear its muted roar above the sound of the motor.

At Acacia Bay, George nosed the prow up onto the sand, we made the headrope fast to a tree and ran for the car. George dropped us at home and we had hot showers and a dram of whisky each.

Rain has eased to a moderate but steady downpour now. At least I won't have to water the garden for a day or so.

January 18

Still coming down. Columns of misty rain moving down the lake but there's little or no wind and the surface is dull pewter grey. We can only just see the town over the water and Tauhara is blanked out completely.

January 20

Stopped raining at last and this morning was mild and fresh-smelling. Still some broken cloud carried on a light northerly but the sun came through now and then. Garden is well soaked and although the hillside drains quickly I won't need to water for a couple of days. Tomatoes seem to have survived the downpour without any real damage and the pale yellow arrows have broken through on the tips of the sweet corn.

January 21

Took a lovely 4lb hen fish at the mouth of Mapara Stream
this morning, but as I beached her she exuded ripe ova. Six
glistening carnelian spheres lay on the wet sand so I carefully
removed the fly and held her in the flow of the stream inside
the bar. She lay quietly, gills pulsating and then she was
gone upstream in a flash. Hope the rude shock won't prevent
her from observing maternal duties.

Seem to be at least a few fish running the streams to
spawn even at this early stage of the year.

January 23

Called on Jack at Waitahanui today. Took him a smoked fish
and a couple of books he'd asked to borrow. One was my
treasured *Going Fishing* by American journalist Negley
Farson, a classic of fishing literature hard to come by
nowadays outside the libraries. Farson's tight and evocative
journalism covers fishing experiences in many parts of the
globe during his correspondent days. He was never without
his rods and found them in many cases to be a magic entrée
to news stories he might otherwise have missed.

Revolutions, wars and uprisings were all grist to his mill, but opportunities for fishing were never neglected.

As a young man recently married, he spent an idyllic two years in a houseboat on an isolated lake in British Columbia, writing stories and articles for a less than meagre living while supplementing the family diet with rod and gun. Despite the hardships, he recalls it as one of the happiest periods of an adventurous life.

Jack too, has been a great fisherman, but the ravages of time and arthritis keep him from the water nowadays. He's lived at Waitahanui for many years and enjoys the fellowship and good company of his Maori neighbours, many of whom share his opinion of Waitahanui as the prime fishing venue in the Taupo area. Often I tease him about his 'picket-fence' affiliations with the men who stand in line across the rip letting their big lures dart and flutter in the outflow to tempt the spawning winter rainbows or those seeking the cool river water in the heat of summer. He defends his choice fiercely and his dedication is almost as total as that of expatriate Irishman Ernest de Lautour, whose devotion to the river prompted him to build a rough bach on its banks just above the main road bridge in the early years of this century. He paid the local Maori owners an annual rental of two bags of flour.

He fished just about every day, but shortly before the start of World War I, chronic asthma put an end to it. The pool immediately upstream of the main highway bridge bears his name — albeit misspelt as 'de Latour'

January 24

Two fine fish taken on the smelt from the rock groyne at the Waikato outlet this morning. It was grey and still but the strong pull of the outflow gave sufficient movement to mask the deception. A white-throated shag was vying for smelt in the same area, but he wasn't as fast off the mark as the trout and the poor return relative to effort soon discouraged him.

A pair of Welcome swallows seem to be nesting under the eaves of the harbourmaster's office on the wharf. I'd left the car close to the wharf and the pair darted in and out from the eaves with fluffy moustaches of food or nest material, I couldn't tell which. Pretty little birds, blue-black on top with fawn fading to cream on the belly and a chestnut throat and face.

January 27

Bill and his family in Rotorua got the two fish from the groyne. We spent two nights with them and a day with Ken and Meg at Ngongotaha. Ken's vegetable garden is in magnificent shape, far better than ours, and he even breeds his own worms for soil improvement. He showed me some minute egg capsules and the tiny threads of recently hatched

Welcome Swallow

worms, something I've never seen before. These are carefully placed under the rich blanket of compost covering the vegetable beds. He has a crop of rainbow chard, silver beet with stems of bright red, yellow and orange. Bill was delighted with the fish — even though they weren't taken trolling — and one of them was filleted and cooked in his portable box smoker. Very acceptable, but this is cooking rather than smoking and the flavour doesn't seem to go right through.

January 28

Nick not so good today. Some sort of stomach bug I think and she's spent the day in bed. I've been playing housewife and writing a little as well. She didn't eat anything during the day, but tonight found room for mayonnaise shrimps and brown bread and butter together with long-eared cos lettuce and radishes from the garden.

It's hot and I'm out on the sundeck but it's almost too dark to write now. Looking north I can see the white wraiths of thermal steam floating up against the dark background of pines beyond the Wairakei borefield. Herman is lying along the sundeck rail smiling fatly with eyes almost closed. Probably remembering the remains of a smoked trout he had for dinner, laced with the juice from the tin of shrimps.

January 29

Nick back to normal now. Wonder if it was the box-smoked fish? An uncharitable thought and I had no ill effects from it anyway. She did her piece at the radio station this morning and seems quite alright. Rain this afternoon moving in grey vaporous clouds from the south. Might try for smelting fish at Whakamoenga tomorrow morning.

Norman told me he'd hooked the fish at about six this morning on his first cast.

It was nearly eight when I pushed aside the dry rattling broom pods and came out onto the open rocks to see him standing on the point with rod arched and nothing much happening. The big Parsons Glory had only just hit the water he said when a fish took it on the surface and that was the last he'd seen of fish or fly. He offered me the rod and I felt the heavy throbbing resistance but it didn't move one way or the other. We tried a strain from different angles but we couldn't move the fish. So I left him to it after a while and fished into the stiff southerly coming into the point on the other side. Fish were hawking smelt close to the rocks. Landed two and lost two more. I could see Norman, still attached, on the other point, and when I went back with my two fish at quarter-past-ten he was still there. I had to get home but I promised to phone his wife who'd expected him home some time ago.

Norman phoned me in the middle of the afternoon. At half-past-twelve another angler had offered to climb down the rocks and give the line a few sharp tugs in the hope of moving the fish. This was after a launch had taken the rod and steamed slowly out to get a different angle of strain. Various other shifts of position had been tried but without result. The few tugs did have some effect. The nylon leader broke at the fly.

What size was it, I asked him — he'd caught a glimpse of it when it took the fly — 15lb? 16lb?

No, he said, it was bigger than that. Norman has a number of fishing years under his belt and I respect his judgement. Could it have been foul-hooked perhaps? He conceded this was possible but maintained it was first hooked squarely in the mouth. Poor Norman, my heart bleeds for him. If someone ever hooks it again I hope it's him. And I hope he lands it.

February

Waihi

February 2

Rotongaio Lagoon lies some twenty-two kilometres south of Taupo township and we arrived there shortly after seven last night. The margins are muddy and bordered thickly with reeds and raupo and it's home for a variety of marshland birds.

Fishing is almost impossible from the shore except where the stream enters, or where it leaves the lagoon at the lake. We tramped the track to the inlet to find a clear and smooth-flowing run of water opening over a hard bottom. Roy put on a large deer-hair cicada fly and began to fish up into the mouth. I greased my new salmon-pink floating line, tied on a fat Cochybondhu and waded carefully around the perimeter towards the outlet.

A group of five black swan and a dozen or so mallard held to the middle of the lagoon. There was no breeze and the sun's rays slanted across from far away above the Acacia Bay hills.

I disturbed a long-legged pukeko who flashed a white scut as he made off, picking his way through the detritus of bent-over dead reeds. Then I saw something else. A fierce golden eye betrayed the motionless bittern pointing his dagger bill to the evening sky. I stopped and stared but not a feather moved. Bulkier than the heron, buff-brown with darker streaks, the matuka was beloved of fishermen in past years who made deadly lures from his tiger-striped breast plumes. Now he's strictly protected and the use of his feathers forbidden. And still he didn't move. I stepped closer and his eye widened perceptibly. Closer again and his nerve broke at last. With a clatter of wings he struggled through the constricting reeds and was aloft and away with ponderous wing beats, neck tucked well back into the shoulders. I've seen few bittern before and never one in flight.

Waded on looking for a rise but nothing showed. Dropped a 'blind' cast ahead and immediately a small rainbow engulfed the fly, jumped and came off. I dried the fly in the air and cast again. Another small rainbow came to hand and was released. The sun had dipped below the rim of hills and the afterglow burned orange in the sky. Clumsy sedges began to skate the surface and suddenly one disappeared in widening rings. Another rise close to the reeds. Settled the Cochybondhu lightly onto the spot and it disappeared with a slurping sound. I paused, tightened the line and something surged heavily out into the lagoon then doubled back to the reeds. Turning the rod I urged it away from the stems and it came towards me in the near dark shooting past within inches of my wader. The line slackened and I stripped it through the rings to regain contact. He was still on, tugging stubbornly against the pull of the rod. Now he floundered on the surface, made another bid for the centre, stopped and returned unwillingly. Two more powerful runs and then he seemed to give up the battle. Eased him in close, unshipped the folding net and rolled him into it.

Waded back to the inlet, the fish still in the net and stepped up onto the bank. Roy was waiting there with another brown almost identical with mine. We weighed them on the spot and his beat mine by two ounces, pulling the needle of the scale down to 7lb 4oz.

As we stumbled back to the car by the light of a dim torch, a loud reverberating boom sounded from the reeds on our left. I told Roy about flushing the bittern.

'Well, seeing you frightened him,' he said, 'perhaps he thought he'd do the same to you.'

Halfback Nymph

February 4

Saturday and a delightful picnic with Roy and Pam. Drove south to the Waipehi Stream where the open pumice beach abuts the main highway and you can park under the kowhais beside the water. The kowhais' golden bells are long gone but the small dainty leaves remain the year round. Lazed on the beach for an hour, talking and drinking coffee. The sun was bright on the calm water and to the south-west we could see the smoky blue ramparts of Western Bays.

A pair of tuis clambered around the big kowhai above the car, nodding and clacking their bills at each other. Roy put his rod together in a leisurely fashion and waded barefoot into the quiet rip, punching out a small Lord's Killer on a bright green floating line. We admired his style and called out disparagingly when he caught the bottom. He freed the fly, sloshed ashore and changed it for a Half-back nymph. On his third cast across and down the stream mouth his rod arched and a fat rainbow kicked into the air and powered out towards the middle of the lake. We shouted encouragement and various pieces of useless advice but he eventually beached it even so.

Carried out a stomach analysis on the spot and discovered seven or eight smelt, their silver translucency now turned dull white, numerous horny-cased caddis and a large partially digested green caddis creeper.

Caddisfly

We arranged some large pumice pieces in a semi-circle and had a twig and driftwood fire going within minutes. Roy wrapped the fish in four sheets of dampened newspaper and placed it in the glowing embers. In fifteen minutes we were in business. The paper peeled off taking scales and skin with it, leaving the moist flesh pink and hot for the butter, salt and pepper. A side dish of tomato sandwiches completed the meal and we washed it down with a flagon of beer.

February 8

Graham rang early this morning. Could I take an American airline pilot out for the day? His guiding arrangements had fallen through and the visitor had only one day before reporting back to Auckland.

I could and did. He was an excellent fisherman, casting a long and accurate line with my unaccustomed gear. I stood back under the trees calling the shots as he covered smelting fish in the grey heaving chop at Te Kumi Bay. He hooked four, landed two and came ashore soaking wet and happy as a sandboy.

Dried him off at home, put a drink and some lunch into him and saw him off in a rental car in the afternoon. He presented me with a dozen of his own beautifully tied dry flies and promised to return on his next New Zealand trip. I hope he does.

February 11

Another visitor today, a friend of Nick's brother Patrick. A beautifully mannered Malaysian student on his way from Wellington to Auckland. He was no fisherman but marvelled at Taupo and its surroundings. 'Like this we have nothing,' he told us with a wondering shake of the head.

Took him to Huka Falls and told him the story of the long-ago Maori chief who drowned his enemy in the racing torrent. On the pretext of 'burying the hatchet', the local chief invited his victim to visit Taupo and sample his hospitality. Well knowing his rival's reputation, the visitor brought a band of warriors with him. He was shown the falls and expressed the opinion that no-one and nothing could live in it. 'Nonsense!' the local chief replied. 'I go down nearly every day in my canoe just for the fun of it.'

The visitor said this was something he'd like to see, but his host insisted that he could only do so if accompanied in another canoe by his guest. The visitor was trapped. If he refused he would lose 'mana' in front of his own and the other chief's men. So the two canoes were brought into the pool above the rapids, the two chiefs took their places and were soon sucked into the deadly vortex of the falls. Less than halfway down, local warriors hidden on either side of the falls threw a rope across to lift their chief to safety. At the same time others fell upon the visiting warriors and slaughtered them to a man. The other chief disappeared into the roaring maelstrom of the falls and the canoe smashed to splinters.

Our own guest received more thoughtful treatment and spent the night with us before catching the coach to Auckland.

February 13

Weather much improved now. Sweet corn cobs swelling on thick green stems and the golden cornsilk is showing. Should brown up in two weeks and then we'll be breaking it off and rushing them straight away into the boiling pan. This is the only way to cook corn. Every second from plant to pan counts.

February 14

Received a St Valentine's card today. It had a Taupo postmark and I'm sure I know the writing. Nick's show of jealousy pretty transparent. Why don't I think of these things?

February 18

Spent a couple of hours with Nick at Whakaipo Bay yesterday afternoon. Flat calm, brilliant sunshine and the place to ourselves. Nick sat on the beach reading and swatting sandflies while I wandered around the left of the stream with the rod, but not with hope.

Just this side of the big willow on the point, two Captain Cooker piglets erupted from the lupin and skidded to a halt as they saw me. Instinctively lifted the rod and aimed at one but couldn't find a trigger. The piglets turned and bolted back into the scrub squealing for mother and I heard her deep grunt as she called them in. Crashed into the lupin after them but they were away and gone into the dense manuka.

Stumbling and sliding back along the rocky foreshore I arrived breathlessly to report to Nick. I was all for racing back home for the rifle but more moderate counsels prevailed. 'Leave it until early tomorrow morning,' she suggested, 'they'll still be in the area.' And so I was persuaded.

We were leaving shortly before five when old John arrived, ready to prepare himself for the evening's fishing. He chided me for leaving when I should be starting, but I told him we'd had enough and Nick was suffering with the sandflies. We said nothing about the pigs. Arrived there before six this morning, left the car well back up the hill and walked down to the lake. A pearly mist-filled morning with the sun still tucked behind the Kaimanawas. Dew glistened on my boots as I mounted the stile above the stream mouth. The .22 Hornet held a full clip of five hollow-point shells.

Turned off before the beach and tracked through the wet fern well back from the shore. As I drew level with the stand of lupin where I'd seen the pigs, a hoarse bark shattered the morning calm. The scrub parted and a stocky, shark-jawed pig dog wagged his stump of a tail at me. Heard voices and along the track came old John with another man and two more dogs. John was trailing a rifle and his mate carried a small fat boar over one shoulder and a piglet in the other hand. John told me he'd heard pigs in the scrub while fishing the stream mouth three nights ago and this was the morning he'd decided to have a go at them.

I behaved with admirable restraint if I say so myself. We chatted civilly enough for a while then I left them and walked back along the shore to the stream mouth. A slight breeze riffled the surface of the lake and fish were beginning to broach after smelt. My rod was at home. The counsel of women is not always to be relied upon.

February 21

Completely overwhelmed this morning. I'd forgotten it was my birthday but Nick hadn't. Suppose it's a sign of advancing age — on my part I mean.

The frying pan wall clock's bright copper face glows handsomely against the stained timber of the living-room. Had a bottle of wine with our lunch, then listened again with great enjoyment to the Schubert sonata in G major with the brilliant Ashkenazy on piano — a present from Nick's family which arrived in the post this morning.

Stayed up late listening to a radio play which featured Nick and finally turned in after midnight. A lovely day.

Himalayan Honeysuckle

Lupin

February 22

We lay spreadeagled looking over the grass ridge at the tall stand of native bush across the gully. The fenceline cut a clean division between forest and pasture and six or seven rabbits were feeding close to the fence. We'd been there for more than half an hour and now the last rays of sun drew back along the lake a mile down the sharp ridges to our left. Magpies tumbled and argued in a high rimu and a portly bronze-wing pigeon launched himself to plane off down the valley.

It was cooler now but nameless insects crawled up and down my bare legs and it was hard to lie still. The 30.06 was still sun-warm under my hand, the safety catch already off. Michael lay still some yards away, his hawklike profile intent on the fenceline scrub. More rabbits were feeding now and he was aching for a shot.

Fifteen minutes passed and my eyes began to smart. It was still light but detail was becoming fuzzy. Michael looked across and nodded, then slowly inclined his head towards the forest. Now I saw movement in the fern and a big black sow shambled halfway out of the foliage and snouted the air. We were downwind and she couldn't cut our scent.

Two more shouldered out of the fern and all three began to root the grass along the fenceline. Slowly levelling the rifle over the peak of the ridge I homed in on the third pig, a fat young sow with white rump patches. Centred on the shoulder, held my breath and took the first trigger pressure. Full side-on, a perfect shot. Squeezed harder and the shocking blast was echoed by the flat crack of Michael's .22. The sow fell on her side, all four legs thrashing convulsively. The other two bolted into the scrub, the magpies gargled in panic and flashed away up valley. And one rabbit kicked its last on the near side of the fence.

The shot had taken her in the neck, completely severing the spine. I'd shot too high but at least the foreleg was undamaged and I'd tell Nick I had aimed for the neck. We bled and gutted her, took out the liver and kidneys, then grabbed a back leg each and dragged her to the car. We spread newspaper in the boot, heaved her inside and drove back to the caravan.

Knocked off a bottle of good Hawke's Bay white wine betweeen us and then I drove home.

February 23

Dressing and butchering pigs isn't my favourite pastime. With George's help this morning I built a flat fire of dead broom and manuka in the empty section and we singed off the coarse black hair. I honed up the skinning knife and scraped the hide free of remaining bristle, then we scrubbed it clean with soap and hot water and hosed it down inside and out. George is a much better butcher than me and he had it dismembered in record time. He has a bigger deep-freeze than ours too, so now most of it is bedded down there and we have a foreleg and the offal in ours. I'll have one ham cured in town. The whole operation isn't as clean a job as scraping in the bath of hot water but much less trouble.

Horopito – Flowers Sept. Fruit Feb.

High ramparts of cliff enclose Kaiapo Bay. It's small, secluded and gets little sun. No-one else goes there and I don't often fish it myself. The farmer who owns the land gives me free passage and I usually give him a fish on the way back if I get onto them.

It's forbidding and gloomy and the thick stand of native bush creeps almost to the stony shore. It never seems to get the wind and today was no exception. But the shoreline falls away suddenly and a lure in the deep water almost always draws a fish or two. Landed four today but the melancholy atmosphere inspires morbid thoughts and I didn't enjoy it very much.

The story I was told about the place accords with its sombre ambience. Two fencing contractors once rented the existing farmhouse. One day one of them found an old Maori skull tucked in a cleft of rock in the cliff face by the bay. He took it home and despite protests from his wife and Maori partner, he kept it on a shelf in the kitchen as a curiosity. Then things started to happen.

He awoke one night for no reason and looked out of the bedroom window. By the light of a fitful moon, intermittently obscured by racing clouds, he saw a war party of a dozen Maori warriors in full regalia up along the homestead fence gazing in at him. Within seconds they were gone.

A few days later his wife miscarried with their first child, and a week after that his partner broke a leg and was off work for six weeks. Working laboriously on his own, the fencer fell and smashed out his front teeth on the end of a fencepost. A local dentist attended to him and was told the story of the skull which, by this time, was causing the fencer some apprehension.

The dentist, a collector of Maori artefacts and antiquities, offered to give the skull a home in his own collection and his offer was readily taken up. Within two weeks the dentist died of a heart attack, a relatively young man with no previous record of illness.

The fencer took the hint, recovered the skull from the dentist's widow and replaced it where he'd found it. No more mishaps occurred during his remaining two years on the property.

As I say, the fishing is nearly always rewarding but I don't often go there.

February 26

This is usually the hottest month of the year but already there's an edge to the wind. Smelting is tailing off whereas sometimes they're still at it in early April.

But the sweet corn is well set and there'll be warm weather yet. March can sometimes be a wonderful month but that cold edge to the wind makes me wonder about this year.

February 27

Tried the first of the sweet corn this evening. The cobs were snapped off and in the boiling water within seven minutes. Simmered for five minutes more, then we took them out, splashed them briefly with cold water and applied the butter and pepper and salt. You don't have to chew it off when it's like this. Merely run your teeth around them and let the succulent seeds drop into your mouth. It's a messy business but well worth it. Nick had four and I demolished five.

Karapapa

February 28

Still warm but the air is sharp and clear. This morning the mountains eighty kilometres to the south stood out boldly against a pale blue sky. Tonight the lake is silk-smooth and Tauhara lies black and dense, dreaming above the winking lights of the town.

March

Whakaipo

March 2

Nick looks after the flowers. I don't do much in this area but I enjoy seeing them around. By the same token she enjoys my vegetables.

We have a brave display through her efforts this year. The rockery below the sunporch is a smother of colourful pansies, deep purple and yellow, their little child-faces smiling up at the sun. Around the back door the pink sweet william has done its dash for the season, but now salvias have mustered forces for a scarlet takeover bid.

Nick loves her roses and while I like to see them glowing against the dark-stained timber I have reservations about the cruel thorns that snag me when I'm weeding. Our thornless banksia rose is my special favourite. The tight yellow blooms are gone now, but in spring, they spread butter-yellow up the northern wall in lovely contrast with the bright mauve of the flowering virgilia close by.

Nick has an attractive cartwheel arrangement of herbs beside the main vegetable patch, each mass of plants

89

separated by spokes of pumice stones. She uses them fresh for cooking, and there's oregano, thyme, basil, tansy, rosemary, bergamot, chives, parsley and a few others we're not too sure about. And of course catnip, Herman's favourite, predictably. He grazes it delicately from time to time and acts very strangely afterwards.

Today I cut back the creeping growth of Queensland Blue pumpkin threatening to invade the herb garden. Its heavy globes are lurking in the long grass swelling day by day to make rich soup when the cold weather comes.

March 4

Today the face of the lake, smiling and benign for many days, changed to a vicious snarl.

The morning was bright and clear with no warning of what was to come. High cumulus lifted above the triple peaks at the lake's southern end and a light breeze soon cleared the early mist. But by lunchtime the complexion of the lake had changed. Cloud descended, pressing down in the east and a fitful wind bowed the poplars on the point. Soon it strengthened and began to roar in the pines behind the house, scarring the lake with white racing foam. It seemed to come from everywhere at once. Wide patches of the surface spread and flattened as though from the blades of a giant helicopter. Garden trees thrashed in the whistling wind and squalls of driven rain peppered the house like birdshot.

Sometimes we get these sudden storms and often there's little warning. George, an old seaman, tells me he feels far safer at sea than on the lake. The ocean gives you plenty of forewarning, he says, but Taupo catches you unawares.

One family will remember today. On the early news tonight we heard that a man had drowned during the storm. A visiting weekender from Wellington fishing with a friend off the Horomatangi Reef. They hadn't been quick enough to heed the signs and the boat swamped and overturned. The friend floated in his life-jacket and eventually struggled ashore. But the dead man wasn't wearing one.

Now, in the near dark, the wind has died too but the lake rolls and heaves uneasily in the aftermath of the storm.

March 8

Only a few of us fish the Boulevard. It's fast, broad and shallow for the most part, unsuitable for the downstream lure through much of its length. Lure fishermen usually by-pass it on the way from the Major Jones Pool and the swing bridge up to the Neverfail and Kamahi Pools.

I fish it upstream with nymph and floating line and the water holds some good browns, probably as many as any comparable pool on the Tongariro. The problem is to get them out. You have to be right in the water for a start and the bottom is mainly greasy rocks from cannonball up to small car size. So you get in, balance yourself against the strong thrust of the river and drop your nymph above or in the pockets and eddies behind the jutting boulders. Then you gather line fast as the shifting currents slide it down towards you. So you move on, slipping, slithering, staggering, casting as you go.

Kingfishers haunt the close overhang of macrocarpa and willow on your right, dipping swiftly to snatch cockabullies from the slower water by the bank. Song thrushes are there too and the little grey warbler.

Lost three good fish this morning, one brown and two rainbow, because I let them take me downstream and I couldn't follow, stuck teetering precariously between two boulders in the heavy water. Sometimes, when they start to go down, I throw loops of line quickly downstream to try and fool them to go up against the rod and the push of the river. But you have to be quick — quicker than I usually am.

Did better after lunch, rolling a fat brownie into the net

after keeping a strain from below for ten long minutes. Then a rip-roaring rainbow broke me sixty or seventy yards downstream. Towards the head of the Boulevard I hooked another and managed to steer him into the net after a long fight. Scooping him up I lost my footing and went under up to the chin and it was cold, cold, cold. Sloshed ashore, still with the fish, took off the chest waders and emptied them, then squelched back along the track to the car in stockinged feet. Another fisherman came along the track going the other way. He looked me up and down, smiled and gestured at the two fish. 'Hey they're pretty good. But it looks as though you got them snorkelling.'

March 13

Took the long-promised trip to Lake Otamangakau with John today — much against Nick's better judgement.

It's not attractive fishing, a man-made hydro-storage lake way up beyond Lake Rotoaira. But the fish, when you strike them, are magnificent. We were lucky. Fishing a deep sunken chironomid nymph into the lake from near the boat ramp, I took two lovely rainbows, the better one almost 6½lb. John took a 5-pounder and lost two more, one of which might have gone 8lb. It took him down to the last few turns of backing, then leapt splendidly before throwing the hook.

It's a bare and featureless landscape. Low tussock and heath surround the wide perimeter and a keen wind is an almost contant reminder of the altitude. Red-billed gulls mew piteously overhead and the pied stilts leave a criss-cross of prints on the silt margins. There's a multitude of insect life in and around the lake. Dragon-flies abound, often snatched out of the air by opportunist fish as they skim the surface locked in nuptial flight.

No smelt in Otamangakau as far as I know, and very few cockabullies, and yet the trolling boats take fish with spinners and lure flies. Surely a firm indication that rainbows will strike at any sort of moving lure even though they're not used to a small fish diet.

Nick seemed glad to see me back in one piece. John stayed for a couple of drinks and we bored her with the details of our day.

March 16

Most trollers aren't fly fishermen. Consequently they fail to realise that their raised voices can often be heard above the chuckle of their outboards by those on shore. On the other hand the close proximity of the motor prevents them hearing much else and they bumble along blissfully unaware that they can be overheard.

Today was a case in point. I fished the southern face of Whakamoenga Rocks with Roy this afternoon. We'd each landed a fish before the boat appeared around the navigation light point. Two men, holding a trolling rod apiece, looked over at us from a hundred yards away.

'Look at those two mugs' one said. 'They'll be dam' lucky to get anything there.' The other nodded. 'Beats me. How they can stand there hour after hour I don't know. Tried it once and never got a touch.'

Almost before he'd finished speaking Roy was hard into a fish. He proceeded to play it with perhaps a little more dramatic flourish than usual. The two trollers watched in silence until the fish was in the net.

'Bit lucky, eh?' one of them said. Before the other could reply, his reel screamed and he struck vigorously at a rock on the bottom.

During the next ten minutes, as they laboriously manoeuvred their craft to free the lure, I hooked and landed a second fish. They reeled in the broken line before continuing on course while we ostentatiously picked up our four fish and made off — to the other side of the point.

March 17

Lunched at Hatepe today, Nick, the dog and myself. We left Turangi at midday after completing some minor business, bought filled rolls and lemonade at the store and spread ourselves beside the stream where the dark-stained water curves and twists between the dense manuka and poplars above the road bridge.

It was hot and still. Nick dabbled her feet in the water and Brodie mooched around in the shallows biting at floating rubbish and water-boatmen. Two little grey warblers flirted in the riverside trees, piping high and shrill. Never still for a moment they flashed white and brown among the interlaced branches, swooping down briefly to pick something from the surface. We looked more closely and discovered a tiny armada of mayflies sailing the polished surface. The sun struck rainbow hues from their gossamer wings.

These are some of God's most beautiful creatures. Ephemeroptera is the name of the insect order and their

94

lifespan is ephemeral indeed, rarely lasting longer than one or two days. We bent close to watch them drift by, tiny legs pricking the surface film of the water, veined wings held high above delicately segmented pale grey bodies arching up from the thicker head and abdomen. Continuing the arch of the body, three slender filaments formed the graceful tail.

A few yards upstream we saw the nymphs rising from the bottom to struggle in the surface film. The hair-like legs work furiously, extending and contracting, then the nymphal shuck splits along the back and the fly emerges. Within seconds the sun dries the crumpled wings, they extend upright above the body and the perfect fly rides high on the shining stream. The metamorphosis is complete.

The flies leave the water to dance and mate in mid-air, then the female dips the surface to lay her fertilised eggs and soon they're back on the water, wings laid flat, spent and dying to be taken by trout or the watchful birds. The minute heavier-than-water eggs sink and are buried in the silt and gravel of the stream bed, ready to continue the changeless cycle for the coming year.

Nick has never seen this delightful phenomenon before and she was fascinated. Brodie snapped a few from the surface but found them an insubstantial snack.

March 18

George brought us some venison backsteaks today. Up in the state forest yesterday morning early, he'd roared up a young stag who was looking for a fight and dropped it with one shot from across a narrow gully. It was too heavy for him to carry out so he'd taken the two haunches, the liver and the backsteaks. Ours are hung in the meatsafe and will stay there for the next five days or so. Then we'll marinate them in red wine before grilling.

March 20

Weed is bad at Whakaipo now. Thick, evil-smelling blankets of it foul the shore on either side of the stream mouth and bloated cockabullies float dead in the shallows.

Today the sun baked a thin crust on its surface and I could smell it as soon as I left the car. Even the hardy koura aren't proof against the oxygen-stealing decay and their blue-shelled carapaces lie flaccid on top of the weed.

Trudged around beyond the willow point where the shoreline began to clear and pitched a small green smelt onto the ruffled surface. A black shag, hanging his wings out to dry on the big rock further round, begrudgingly lifted off, leaving his orange and white spattered perch to observe me from further out in the lake. The far off whine of a light aircraft blasted suddenly loud and I looked around to see the small plane spreadeagled briefly against the sky above the Kaiapo bluff. A thick brown band of fertiliser spewed from its white belly to fall in a cloud on the unseen pasture below. The plane disappeared and the blaring assault of its engine diminished to a nasal whine.

This is the main cause of the build-up of weed. Commercial interests plug the over-use of fertiliser and eventually a hard pan builds up under the pasture. In many cases further applications can't get through and the excess superphosphate runs off with the rain into the nearest river or stream. The enriched water carries on to the lake and promotes unnatural growth of blanket weed, and eutrophication occurs. The simple equation of too much fertiliser = wasted money = overenriched lakes would seem easy to follow, but many people are hard to convince, especially if they have a vested interest.

Spent more than an hour trying for a fish but came away empty-handed. I'd like to blame the weed — it makes a good scapegoat — but doubtless other factors were involved.

March 21

Relented and gave Whakaipo another chance today. A moderate southerly buffeted into the bay bringing intermittent rain. I like these conditions at Whakaipo and the results justified my confidence. Half a mile round from the stream mouth, fish were working smelt in the little bay. Got soaked to the skin breasting the waves but came back with five good ones for the smoker.

Smelt are lasting well after all this year but they're bound to taper off within a week or so. The atmosphere is cooling and the evenings beginning to draw in. The poplars above the stream mouth are showing rust among the green.

March 23

Whitikau Stream joins the Tongariro at the last legal fishing point upstream and the confluence is a likely spot for a fish.

Today John was hosting his friend Maurice from Wellington, a relative newcomer to trout fishing. We'd heard that one of the early spawning runs had reached this far so Maurice was placed at the head of the Sand Pool, armed with a Red Setter and given his riding instructions. John went down to the head of the Blue Pool and I walked up to the fast rocky reach where the Whitikau flows in.

The Pheasant Tail nymph took a fish at the first cast, a nickel-bright hen not long from the lake. She gave me anxious moments before I beached her, then I floundered in again, placing the nymph well over in the fast water towards the centre. Immediately another fish struck, again a fresh-run hen but slightly smaller than the first.

Felt I could afford a break after such a promising start so I sat on a boulder smoking a cigarette, admiring the lovely silver fish arranged fetchingly on a flat rock. A cacophony of sparrows argued and flustered up and down the opposite cliff face. There must have been thirty or forty of them. Strange to see them so far from an urban environment, but they're obviously nesting here raising the last broods of the season. High above the cliff and the tangle of trees, a ragged-winged harrier planed wide circles against a patch of blue sky. Certainly his telescopic vision could pick out the potential below but he'd need a much clearer target if he was looking for lunch.

Struck nothing for the next hour. Went downstream to find Maurice ecstatic with a fine 3½lb jack on the stones. He'd had two other strikes, he said, in the deep eddy opposite the cliff.

Ate our sandwiches together and I went on downstream. John had taken two fish from the Blue Pool and was trying for a third he could see hugging the bottom. 'Been trying for half an hour but I can't shift it,' he told me. 'Why don't you have a go?'

I waded in and began to cast against the freshening downstream breeze. On the third cast the line checked and John shouted 'He has it!' I struck and the rod bent in a throbbing arc. It played well up into the eye of the pool, tugging viciously and shaking its head against the pull of the nymph. Eventually it came ashore under the nodding toi-toi and John hefted it onto the bank. A beautiful leopard-spotted brown which registered 6½lb on the steelyard.

We covered her with leaves and a branch of manuka beside the track and went upstream to collect Maurice. He'd had nothing further so we started the tramp back to the Poutu bridge and the car. I started pontificating to Maurice about fish not always being where one expected them. As we reached the spot where the brownie was hidden I held up a hand and we stopped. 'Now this looks a likely place.' Diving off the track I uncovered the fish and held it up. 'There...who'd have thought to find one here?'

Maurice nodded. 'Very clever, I'm sure. I suppose in that sort of location you must have taken it on a dry fly?'

March 25

Awakened last night by a frightful noise on the roof. Brodie joined in to add to the turmoil so I struggled out of bed, blearily reaching for the dressing-gown and torch.

It was cold outside and a clammy mist blanked out the nearest houses. The beam of the torch picked out what I'd expected, an opossum, walking casually along the guttering. He stopped and stared into the glare of the torch. My immediate thought was to get the small rifle and blast him off the roof, but I decided this would do nothing for neighbourly relations. Picked up two or three rocks from the garden, sighted along the torch beam and let fly. The clatter of the rocks on the roof was worse than the opossum itself but seemed to have the right effect. He set off at a bow-legged run to the northern corner of the house and took a flying leap into the virgilia. He showed no signs of returning so I went back inside, calmed the dog and returned to bed.

Reminded me of the opossum Ken and myself met at the Lake Tarawera fishing lodge some years ago. Testing the quality of a bottle of Scotch shortly after arrival, we were surprised by an opossum elbowing himself up onto the window sill. We hastily shut the window and he then raised himself on hind legs, hung from the top window frame scrabbling on the glass with his back feet. This unnerving

spectacle continued for five minutes or more then he dropped out of sight onto the verandah. We cautiously opened the door a crack and he immediately tried to barge his way in. We put our shoulders to the door, locked it and had a further drink to boost our morale. Our would-be visitor soon resumed his anxious vigil at the window until a man's voice was heard outside. The opossum plopped onto the verandah and was gone.

Later we learned that he belonged to the lodge proprietor and had an unfortunate social problem — alcoholism. Sometime in his youth he'd been introduced to the demon whisky and his master had compounded the evil habit by lacing his daily milk. He was well known by habitués of the camp, who likewise offered his favourite tipple from time to time. His keen nose could detect the whiff of whisky from afar and he was frequently to be seen stumbling around the lodge after dark, muttering and complaining to himself in drunken stupor.

We learned afterwards that he eventually came to a sticky end. One night, with much drink taken, he was too befuddled to avoid an oncoming car and so joined his thousands of more temperate bretheren who immolate themselves on New Zealand roads every night.

March 26

Ruapehu and Ngauruhoe wear mantles of brilliant white today. The atmosphere is crisp and clear and a fresh southerly wrinkles the sapphire blue of the lake. There's a keen edge to the breeze and the smell of autumn in the air.

We've nearly finished the sweet corn and the remaining tassels have all turned from pale gold to brown. Plums are long gone but we're eating the Golden Delicious apples. Beside the vegetable garden the solid chunky crackajack marigolds still hold out in dazzling orange and yellow, and the geranium burns scarlet against the mahogany of the eastern wall. Split some kindling earlier today and we'll have our first fire tonight.

March 28

Rain last night but sharp and bright again today. Worked at the typewriter in the morning clearing up bits and pieces long overdue.

Distracted for at least half an hour before lunch watching a pair of tuis sipping nectar from the red-hot pokers. They grasp the stems firmly, poking long beaks into the narrow blooms and clambering awkwardly from plant to plant. The sun strikes a green–bronze patina from the glossy black feathers and the white chin flags nod and tremble as they feed. Herman watches from the closed window with single-minded concentration. Ornithology is one of his great interests, especially if he can observe at close quarters. But the door is closed too.

March 30

Te Kumi Bay gave me two fish this morning. Both took the green smelt. But the shoals of tiny fish are no longer close in. Their spawning is done and now they're returning to deep water until the margins of the lake warm up again in early December.

Cockabullies still dart and hover in the shallows, prey for the stalking heron by day and the foraging trout after dark. The pale blue koura are there too, but you don't see them during daylight hours.

Tui

April

Waitahanui

April 1

An appropriate day for taking Brodie fishing. Nick thought the outing would do her good — the dog that is — so we accompanied each other to Whakamoenga Rocks where she duly fell in twice and had a near heart attack from the excitement of my only fish.

She's nothing like Murphy. He's Roy's dog, an unkempt, miserable-looking wire-haired terrier who is treated far better than he would have you believe. But he really is a fishing dog. When Roy hooks a fish he watches the play with close and professional concentration. On command he'll cross his front paws and dive gracefully into the lake. Watching for his chance he clamps the fish firmly across the middle and swims ashore to drop it at Roy's feet.

He's equally at home as a mobile landing net on the river. One evening some time ago, Roy decided to fish a certain pool on a river not far from Taupo. Murphy went with him and they arrived at dusk. Unfortunately two other fishermen had beaten them to the pool. Since there was room for only two rods on the pool, Roy made his way, unnoticed by the other two anglers to another part of the river. As he was leaving one of them suddenly shouted, 'I've got one on!' and this was followed by the music of a hard-pressed reel. Murphy's ears pricked and he vanished into the darkness.

Moments later the lucky angler gave voice again: 'Hey, it's a helluva big fish, I can't hold it!' Further sounds of battle ensued followed by the plaintive cry, 'Dammit! I've lost it!'

Roy crept discreetly away through the scrub. Further down the river he came on a group of youngsters enjoying a barbecue. His arrival coincided with Murphy's but was far less dramatic. The dog trotted into the firelight, dripping wet, with a 4lb rainbow trout hanging from his jaws. He was greeted with enthusiasm. It's not every dog who brings his own tucker to a barbecue.

I doubt that Brodie will ever aspire to Murphy's expertise. I should be so lucky.

April 3

Gusting blasts from the north-west bringing low cloud and whiffs of sulphur from Wairakei borefield. The starlings blow like fluttering leaves in the wind and the dead leaves themselves press hard against the wire-netting of the vegetable garden. The March winds do blow on this side of the equator too.

Herman springs high in the air, trying to snatch the whirling leaves, his ears askew and tail lashing in a frenzy of excitement. His eyes glare mad yellow as he hurls himself around the lawn. From the French window Brodie watches him with head on one side. She's unaffected by wind madness and much prefers it inside.

Stonefly

April 5

A pale corona around the sun. No more wind and the lake is calm, but there's a bite to the air. The blue haze smudging the southern mountains has nothing to do with heat. At the point, the golden poplar leaves rock gently down to settle on the calm water.

April 6

I never promote myself as an expert, because I'm not. But sometimes a bit of help at the right time can make a difference to someone else. Down on the beach this morning in front of the lodge, a young fellow was wrestling with the first of two fish he'd brought in from trolling Jerusalem Bay. He was making a dreadful hash of gutting and was coated with blood and slime up to his elbows. I wandered down to compliment him on his catch and he admitted he was new to the game and wasn't too sure of the correct procedure. I said I'd be happy to help and he invited me to demonstrate on the other fish. The first was already a lost cause.

There's a simple way to gut a fish and I showed him how to go about it. Someone showed me years ago and I was glad of it, so I didn't feel patronising.

You poke the point of a sharp knife into the vent and slit the belly right up to the angle of the lower jaw. The blood will flow at this stage if you've done it right. Then press the gill plates together to depress the tongue and cut the membrane between it and the lower jaw so that the tongue hangs free. Hook your left thumb in the lower jaw, grasp the tongue with thumb and fingers of the other hand and pull down. Gills, guts and the lot should come away easily in one piece. Slit the backbone membrane and with a fingernail, push out the liver which lies close along the spine. This job should be finished off with a toothbrush — preferably not your own — and the whole carcase washed clean inside and out. If you have to keep it for a while before going home wrap it well in leaves or grass. If you want to scale your fish, do it before gutting, it's much easier that way.

The young man thanked me and we chatted for a while. He was on holiday from Auckland and he was a doctor. Obviously they don't teach all aspects of anatomy at medical school these days.

April 9

A dozen fresh eggs from George's hens yesterday. Absolutely marvellous and nothing like the plastic shop variety. They're brown with darker speckles, Rhode Island Reds I think, and the yolks are rich orange.

Only six left now; we had four scrambled this morning — made my way. Nick has this strange method which she obstinately swears by. Consists of putting in the butter after the milk and eggs. Very weird. As all connoisseurs know, you put in the knob of butter first, add milk when it's melted, then the eggs and keep stirring slowly with a wooden spoon. Just before it starts to firm up, in go salt, ground black pepper, and chopped parsley. A pinch of chopped chives too if you feel like it and you're in business. Serve it on toast with a few small freshly picked tomatoes.

Actually, hers tastes quite good usually, but I feel the correct principles should be observed if you're going to the do the thing properly. Must do something about getting some hens of our own.

April 10

Card from Guam today. Gene is sweltering in tropic heat, dreaming of Taupo and his Alaskan rivers.

Nothing tropical about Taupo at the moment. A keen wind bustles the whitecaps south, pulling a mournful grey cloud like a blanket over the lake.

April 13

Fish mostly in splendid fettle now, sleek and bright and strong, revitalised by a solid diet of green beetle, smelt and koura. They're in the rivers now, early spawners thrusting up to dig their redds in the cold clean gravel of the headwaters.

Took a brace at the mouth of the Mapara Stream this morning early. A cock and a hen almost identical in size. Both were firm and plump but the hen's small neat head is very different from the larger, hook-jawed profile of the male.

Major Jones Pool

Fishermen are a conservative lot on the whole. The majority of Taupo anglers either troll from power boats or fish the large lure on sinking fly lines in the deeper water of the lake or in the rivers when the fish are running to spawn.

But a quiet revolution has been under way recently, and I'm one of the revolutionaries. We fish the nymph — and sometimes even the dry fly — upstream to the river-running fish. In spite of what the traditionalists think, running fish take the nymph eagerly, quite often more eagerly than the downstream lure.

Yesterday afternoon was cool and bright at the Major Jones Pool. Nick sat reading with her back to a rock at the tail of the pool, well-wrapped in a scarf and my sheepskin. Sometimes on a weekday you're lucky enough to have the pool to yourself, but not very often. Today there was one fisherman way up at the head of the Major Jones. The Tongariro was in lovely order, clear and strong with just a touch of milky blue.

Climbed into thigh waders and began to pitch a Pheasant Tail nymph up into the fast water. Soon a good fish took me deep in the middle then threw the hook as it hit the rapids and leapt almost opposite Nick. Turned round and shrugged and she waved a sympathetic hand. As I worked up, the other man fished down towards me. When we were some thirty yards apart I left the water and came out onto the boulders. He looked at me for a moment then reeled in and came ashore. 'Doing any good?' he asked.

I shook my head. 'Just lost one downstream though.'

He was a big man in his late fifties and and looked like a farmer. 'Had a couple this morning early,' he told me, 'but they seem to be right off now.'

 Pheasant Tail Nymph

We passed the time of day for a few minutes more, then he returned to the water and continued fishing downstream. I went in again above him. Before I had my first cast out he hailed me and I glanced back.

'Hey, d'you know you're fishing in the wrong direction?'

I raised a hand in acknowledgement and began to cast. Landed two fish and lost another towards the head of the pool, then three more anglers appeared so I walked back to collect Nick. The downstreamer had disappeared.

April 16

The wide palmate leaves of the courgettes are mottled and dying after last night's frost. They won't be producing any more now so I dug them up and chopped them onto the compost heap. Frost bit into the pumpkins too, so the serpentine hidden growth was pulled out of the long grass and went the same way. But we have twelve of the big elephant-skinned globes stored away in the garage and tonight Nick will make soup for the first time this year.

She cuts it into chunks, steams off the skin, adds water and mashes the orange lumps to pulp with onions browned in butter, seasoning and a pinch of nutmeg. Then she simmers the lot for an hour or so. Wonderful stuff. I usually eat two full bowls and don't feel like much else.

April 17

Soup was magnificent. Had some for lunch today as well, then thinned out parsnips and leeks. Onion tops have browned off well so I pulled about three dozen and strung them from the beams in the garage alongside the garlic. Carrots are set for use well into the winter and this afternoon I cleaned up the summer vegetable patch and laid a thick mulch of compost. Must take the trailer up to the stables tomorrow for a load of horse manure.

April 20

Silver birch leaves are brown and dry now. Soon they'll all be gone and the fruit trees too will be stark and bare. But we still have the green of the shiny five-fingers, and the kowhai and koromiko keep their leaves all year. The poplars on the point burn gold in the pale sunlight but by the end of the month their leaves will be rotting on the bottom of the lake.

April 22

Heard about a good example of the 'revolution' in action today. Graham arrived at the main road bridge over the Hatepe on Thursday, hoping to get a couple of fish on the nymph. Three anglers were camped on the river beside the first pool above the bridge. One of them was working down the pool and Graham waited until he'd finished.

'Do you mind if I have a go?' he asked. The other man shook his head.

'Help yourself. I can't do anything with them. We've been here for nearly three days and we've only got six between us.'

In went Graham, flicking the nymph upstream on a floating line. In less than a hundred yards he landed six good fish and lost two others. He released them all except one, which he took home for dinner.

April 25

Landed a hen rainbow in beautiful condition at Whakaipo the day before yesterday, a 6-pounder. It was around midday and she took a small Hairy Dog just below the surface. The fight was less than spectacular and I landed her in under six minutes.

Today, in exactly the same place at about the same time the small Hairy Dog made another contact. In its first unbroken run, the fish took me down to the last few turns of backing. My reel carries thirty-five yards of fly line and 150 yards of backing, so let's say it made an unbroken run of 150 yards. Then it leapt twice, seeming to be about half a mile out. It looked like a good fish but was it foul-hooked?

Laboriously winched in line until it was within twenty yards of me. Then it took off again in a searing run as long as the first one. Seventeen minutes from the strike (I timed it) my boot eased it up onto the stones still protesting. A perfect twin of the fish I'd taken two days before, hooked firmly in the mouth.

Can't really account for the difference in spirit. One could theorise that sometimes the hook cuts into a nerve which deadens the response. But just as validly it might hit a nerve which sets the sparks flying. Or could it be a difference in diet? Not in this case I think. The gut of each fish held a few koura remains and nothing else.

Just another of those imponderables I suppose. Fishing would probably be boring without them.

April 26

A brief and violent storm today with sleet in the roaring wind. Got caught at Whakamoenga Rocks, seduced by a mild balmy morning with early mist over the lake.

Had two fish on the rocks and was hoping for a third before going home when the change came. Away south the sky was clear and innocent china-blue. A cold breath on the back of my neck made me turn to see a dense cloud mass coming in fast from the north. A fresh breeze dipped the trees above the rocks and I cursed myself for not bringing the parka.

Moments later the gathering rush of wind came whistling through the trees, a black pall covered half the sky and rain began to hiss on the water. I raced for cover and crouched low under the manuka and five-finger. The cold searching wind thrashed and tore at the scrub. Rain roared on the water now and the lake began to heave and slop against the rocks. Made another dash to the old Maori cave and stood dripping and sodden for some fifteen minutes in the gloomy half light. It was dark as evening outside and the wind moaned in the trees above the cave.

The rain eased slightly, I gathered up rod and fish, toiled panting up the wet track to the car, bundled the gear into the boot and squeezed behind the wheel.

Warm and dry now. The storm has blown itself out but many of our flowers are crushed and flattened by the gale. The evening sky is dark with cloud and the soft rain whispers steadily on the roof.

April 27

A grey and featureless day but the rain has stopped. We spent an hour repairing the damage in the garden, propping up sagging flowers and lopping off splintered branches of five-finger and virgilia. George lost his big virgilia. Blasted flat by the wind it narrowly missed the chicken house. They're a shallow-rooted tree but ours, partially sheltered by the house, suffered no ill effects.

April 29

Dramatic happenings today. Brodie, all unknown to me, was taking her ease under the car when I backed it out of the garage this morning. She fled screaming and yelping under the house and I spent about a quarter of an hour or more crawling on hands and knees, alternately pleading and cursing, before I managed to winkle her out. A wheel had apparently gone over one forefoot. We bundled her into the car and made off at speed to the vet. He X-rayed the foot to find extensive bruising and swelling but no break.

Now she lies mournfully in her basket, gently supported by the forbidden bedroom sheepskin rug. She's had dinner in bed and that has diluted self-pity to some extent. Herman sits primly beside the basket regarding her with enigmatic gaze. He can't quite understand the situation. A tentative swipe at the black nose drew only a deep sigh and a plaintive glance at authority.

April 30

Brodie somewhat recovered today. Limping heavily about the house and milking her misfortune for all it's worth. This evening at dinner-time she shuffled haltingly to the sheepskin-lined basket, crawled in and lay gazing expectantly at the refrigerator. She's obviously on the mend and we hope she's learned something about cars.

Totara

May

The Avenue, Tauranga-Taupo River

May 2

Ring around the moon last night and a pale yellow dawn today with low mist lying in the pockets of the hills. Took a run to the Waikato after breakfast and fished a sunken lure down the fast grey water below the Aratiatia Dam. Not a touch or sign of a fish.

The American Zane Grey camped here during his first trip to New Zealand in 1926, after hunting the marlin and mako shark around the Bay of Islands. He did better than me, but there was no dam then. The renowned writer returned in early autumn the following year accompanied by his brother 'R.C.', son Romer, and his 'major-domo' Captain Mitchell.

The travelling circus comprised three cars and three large trucks full of equipment. They camped at the old Kowhai Pool on the Tongariro, somewhere between the old Duchess and Hut Pools and caught rainbow trout up to 15¼lb. Grey raved about the Tongariro, calling it 'the Athabasca of New Zealand'. He also complained about the number of 'native'

115

Tongariro anglers who used heavy rods and large spoons equipped with equally large treble hooks. At Easter weekend he counted more than three hundred on less than a mile of river close to his camp. Perhaps we're not too badly off today after all.

The efforts of Grey and his friends were somewhat circumscribed by this invasion and he had hard words about riverside manners. In his book, *Tales from a Fisherman's Log* , he describes one young man who 'could only see me as a rich American who wanted all the river to himself. I do not remember exactly what I said then, but am afraid I lost my temper and used some rather characteristic American language. To do him credit he did not swear at me, but he certainly insulted me and my party, and brought to our minds again — for the thousandth time — that Americans are not wanted in New Zealand, except by the better class, who are in the minority.'

Let's hope our bloodlines have improved since then.

May 3

Another quiet windless dawn today. Awakened early by a mellifluous chime of bells. We don't often see the bellbird close to home, or hear him, although occasionally they come to sip the nectar from the red-hot pokers. Got out of bed but couldn't see him anywhere although the sweet chimes continued for some minutes.

Naturalist Sir Joseph Banks, who visited New Zealand with Captain Cook in 1769, wrote that 'they made perhaps the most melodious wild music I have ever heard; almost imitating small bells, but with the most tunable silver sound imaginable.'

A bit of hyperbole perhaps, but it's certainly a sweet sound to greet the new day.

116

May 6

Spent yesterday and the previous night with Pius who had
the bones of a good story for me. With his wife he runs the
sole charge school at a tiny hamlet close to the southern
shore of Lake Rotoaira, which drains the lower slopes of
Ruapehu, and he's newly come to the joys of fishing.
What he lacks in finesse he makes up in enthusiasm, and we
spent five hours on the lake in his runabout. His short and
powerful boat rod would kill a marlin and the huge winch is
equipped with 30lb breaking-strain nylon monofilament.

   After three hours' chugging around Motuopuhi Island,
during which he murdered six unfortunate fish, I persuaded
him to anchor the boat while I worked a small Hamill's
Killer close into the offshore weeds. He watched while I
played and landed two good fish on the light fly gear. Then
his patience ran out. 'Vat for you do all this pretty-pretty
bloddy stuff eh? Why not you just reef de buggers in?'

   I'll have to work on him, I can see. His attitude ill accords
with that of his countrymen who are renowned for the
precision, patience and delicacy of hand required to make the
world-famous Swiss watches.

Makomako - Bellbird

May 8

Pius, the most generous of souls, insisted that I take home five of his six fish together with my own two, and these are now turning golden brown in the smoker. Rotoaira fish are beautiful — not over large but thick and deep and they eat magnificently. George adores them above all others, so two are earmarked for him.

Some years ago I took an American visitor to the outlet of the Poutu River at the northern end of Rotoaira. We fished from the outlet through the 150-yard dog-leg which merges into swampy tussock, covering the course four or five times; he with beautifully controlled light spinning gear and myself with a fly. Throwing our respective lures close into the deep runs under the flax and toi-toi on the far side, we landed sixteen fish between us in less than two hours.

'The boys at home won't believe this,' my friend said. 'And I'm not too damn sure I do myself.'

May 10

The saffron wash of gorse bloom and the butter-yellow broom are gone from the hills behind us now.

Lying under the dark green coverts shortly after dawn today, knees cold from the dew, I missed two easy sitting shots in the space of less than an hour. Misty rain softened the spiky frieze of pines against the sky and as the sun rose above the dim Kaimanawas, a blackbird tried an experimental obbligato from the spreading macrocarpa. Heaved up stiffly from the damp parka, bolted the shell from the Hornet's breech and flicked out the magazine. I was hungry and needed a hot shower.

The lake's surface shone like polished silver and the rain had almost stopped. South, where the clouds still massed dense and grey, a bright rainbow arched above the water. It was easy to imagine the perfect circle continued under the surface, but if so, what price the pots of gold? The clean smell of morning was still in my nose when I opened the door and Nick called sleepily from the bedroom.

'Must be losing my grip,' I called back. 'Missed two sitters. But I can probably still make a cup of tea.'

May 13

Slip Creek burbles quietly into Waihi Bay close to the old Maori village of Waihi at the southern end of the lake. It's the only place other than Rotongaio Lagoon where I've seen bittern, pointing like statues in the camouflage of the roadside reed and raupo.

We spent last night at Barrett's bach, filling up with sausages and fried eggs before braving the calm dark of the stream mouth. John scored twice before I'd had a touch — good fish both, thrashing and twisting onto the stony beach in the beam of the torch. No moon, only freezing stars wheeling in the immensity of sky. The lines sighed and whispered above the endless mutter of the gravel bar and John's cigarette glowed fitfully on my right. On the other side, sparse lights from the little village pricked the darkness and occasionally an unseen fish churned the surface. The water is shallow here but we seemed poised on the edge of a black abyss.

Matuku – Bittern

John's reel spoke again in high pitch and a fish slapped heavily onto the water. It fought strongly but at last I hefted it out with my boot, a handsome 4½lb jack, gasping in the light of the torch. Ten minutes later I made my first contact, a gentle arresting of the moving line followed by a powerful surge straight out into the bay. Landed two more and lost another while John improved his tally by a further two.

At eleven o'clock we reeled in, gutted the fish, strung them on baling twine and made our way by wavering torchlight up the track beside the stream to the road bridge. We made cocoa and toast, then crawled into the sleeping bags at midnight. I was out like a light within moments.

May 15

Sometimes May can be kind. This morning, with Arthur and Merren from Wellington, we took our lunch to Whakamoenga Rocks and sat in the warm sun on the southern face.

A mild sou'westerly ruffled Mine Bay and snow lay brilliant white on the triple peaks eighty kilometres down the lake. I'd brought the rod but more through habit than in hope. 'Aren't you going to give it a try?' Arthur said. 'I want to take some fish back to Wellington.'

I told him it wasn't as easy as that and I could guarantee nothing. But I gave the small Hairy Dog a swim from the narrow point in front of where we were sitting. We had lunch half an hour later and the three fish were stowed in a crevasse out of the sun. With lunch over I went at it again and by two o'clock three more fish had joined the others.

'Well there you are,' I told Arthur. 'A little something for you to take home.'

He was highly gratified. 'I knew the fishing was good at Taupo, but I didn't think it was that easy.'

Nor did I.

May 16

Arthur and Merren left early for Wellington this morning with their six fish. So I went back to the rocks to fill a few holes in the deep-freeze. The sun was warm on the southern face, tempered by a mild sou'westerly. Returned home fishless at half-past three.

May 18

A bright crackling morning after a sharp frost last night. This is my kind of winter weather and typical of Taupo. I don't really care how cold it gets as long as we're warm in bed. Nick has an electric blanket on her side and its proximity is sufficient for my needs.

In the morning the living-room is warm from the banked-up stove and the blower heater soon takes the edge off the bathroom's chill. On mornings like this, Herman, banned from our bedroom, is frequently discovered crammed in beside Brodie in her basket, albeit with some peripheral overhang. He's quite unembarrassed to be found so but Brodie, for some reason, seems to think apologies are in order.

Pihoihoi - Pipit

May 19

Another sparkling cold day. Took a pre-breakfast walk for no reason at all up towards the scrub-covered gully at the top of the road.

Ngauruhoe was putting on a great show of temper, belching out dirty brown smoke to stain the clear sky for miles to the south-west.

Ngauruhoe's fire came from the gods in far-off Hawaiki, the legendary home of the Maori people, so we are told. Ngatoroirangi, high priest and navigator of the Arawa canoe, which landed here nearly seven hundred years ago, was the instigator of the fire.

This forbear of Lake Taupo's Tuwharetoa tribe and also Rotorua's Arawa people, climbed Mount Tongariro to survey and claim the surrounding land. He had told his followers to fast until his return, taking with him only a slave girl, Auruhoe. But his followers broke the fast and in anger the gods sent freezing blizzards and snow which almost killed Ngatoroirangi on the high mountain. The tohunga prayed to his gods in Hawaiki for fire to save his life and, to reinforce his plea, sacrificed the unfortunate Auruhoe. The gods heard him and sent fire underground and under the sea from the homeland. It erupted from White Island in the Bay of Plenty, at Rotorua, and at Taupo to eventually blaze forth from the craters of Tongariro and Ngauruhoe.

Warmed and strengthened, the tohunga tipped the body of the slave girl into the crater's flames, which have burned ever since. Ngauruhoe is still called Auruhoe by the older Maoris of the area.

Tongariro was once the collective name for both peaks and it means 'Carried away on the south wind' like Ngatoroirangi's impassioned prayers to his gods in Hawaiki.

May 21

A short afternoon at Whakaipo, but nothing like the last
time I was there. A cold southerly chopped the waves into
the stream mouth, pushing the flow along the right-hand
shore.

Took two nice winter-bright fish from the willow tree bay
and lost another which set an unstoppable course for the
southern end of the lake. Back at the car, I watched an aerial
dog-fight between a hawk and two magpies far above the
big macrocarpa and stark grey poplars. Pure bravado on the
part of the magpies; their breeding season is long since gone.
The harrier was all for a quiet life by the look of it but the
pied bandits had other ideas. One would climb and dive
from above, missing him by inches while the other harassed
and niggled from below. Tumbling and checking on ragged
wings, the hawk eventually disappeared into the steep gully
below the Kaiapo bluff with his persecutors still in pursuit.

The sky already darkening as I drove up the hill from the
lake and a cold grey mist with rain in its wake came rolling
into the bay from the south.

May 24

Lifted some more onions today and hung them in the
garage. Cold wind continues from the south and we've kept
the stove banked up all day. In the fading light this afternoon
we watched a lonely figure on the right-hand point of Acacia
Bay. Trained the binoculars on it and recognised Frank
lurking under the black parka. Waves sloshed up the rocks
onto his right side and I'm sure he was getting wet despite
the parka. Sooner him than me.

May 25

Spawning fish running in the Tauranga-Taupo today.
Bundled up like Michelin men in body-waders, sweaters and

Kahu - Harrier

parkas, we fished down the fast curving flow of the Crescent into a mean and searching wind. George struck eight fish but landed only four. I took two and lost another on the downward trip, then changed to a floating line and nymph to cover the same ground back upstream. Landed a further four then we called it a day and tramped back to the car beside the gravel crusher. They were lovely fish, sleek and bright from the lake. All bar two went back to continue their journey to the swift shallow redds of the headwaters.

Both of us thoroughly chilled but ever-provident George produced a flask which gave us a welcome glow. Had a hot shower as soon as I got home and now I can feel the heat of the stove on my back as I sit at the desk.

May 27

'That's one of the prettiest steelhead I've seen for quite a while,' Frank said.

124

We stood on the sloping pumice beach at Wharewaka Point looking down at the glistening fish bright as a jewel on the dull sand. The head was small, thickening smoothly to heavy shoulders and the deep flank tapered to a graceful tail. It would have weighed no more than 3lb and there was no suggestion of the rainbow's roseate lateral bar.

Steelhead is the term Taupo anglers apply to maiden fish yet to spawn for the first time. The name recalls the origins of Taupo's trout when ova were shipped from California in 1884, hatched and introduced to the lake. The ova were taken from North American steelhead, the sea-run form of the rainbow which follows the life cycle of the salmon, spending most of its life growing fat and strong on the bounty of the sea before ascending the river of its birth to spawn.

Taupo has no clear outlet to the sea, so the lake is the ocean in microcosm. The rainbow thrives on the rich food supplies of the lake and, towards autumn and during the winter, runs the river to spawn. They colour richly during the upstream run, the cock fish especially, blackening overall and turning blood-red along the flanks. They lose condition rapidly before spawning and many die soon after reproducing.

The remainder drift back to the lake to recover and 'mend' themselves. But the virgin or maiden fish is bright silver without the characteristic rosy blush of the rainbow. Steelhead above 3lb are rare, because heavier and presumably older fish have already spawned once or more. There's the odd exception, the lovely silver fish which may be as much as 5lb, but they are rare indeed and one can only attribute their existence to a gourmand appetite or a moral rectitude found, alas, only too infrequently in these decadent times.

Frank gutted his steelhead and showed me the rich orange flesh of the gut cavity. 'That'll eat like a dream,' he said. 'I'll split it, put on lemon juice, salt, pepper, butter and a few herbs, then poke it under the grill. My word, I'm looking forward to it.'

May 29

A swift visit from Derek today. He's up from Wellington for three days and, being Derek, every available moment must be spent fishing.

I often wonder which gets his most careful attention, his law practice, his family, or fishing. Uncharitable though to work out the priorities because he's a good solicitor and his family seem to want for nothing. But I have my own ideas.

He's been known to camp for a week on his own at some of the Western Bays, eating fish supplemented by meagre rations bought along the road and paying scant attention to matters of dress and hygiene. But as he says himself, fishing has little to do with haute couture, bathing, shaving and brushing the teeth, and he's always a model of propriety and cleanliness in Wellington.

Often he'll leave Taupo in the early hours of a Monday morning to arrive at nine o'clock at his Wellington office, where he keeps a razor and change of clothing.

Sometimes his trips to Taupo are squeezed into a schedule which would appear quite pointless to most people. Like the time he left home late on a Friday night, promising to be back home to attend his daughter's birthday party the following evening. He arrived at Taupo at five on Saturday morning. It was a lovely day but perhaps a bit too bright. By ten he hadn't touched a fish and the sun shone brazenly from a cloudless sky. Lunchtime passed and still he was fishless. At half-past two he gave up the struggle and headed for home. He stopped for petrol at a lakefront garage, where he was told by the proprietor that less than half an hour before, he'd seen fish chasing smelt immediately opposite the service station. Derek looked at his watch. Just for half an hour, that wouldn't make much difference. He hurriedly put up his rod and trotted down to the beach.

It was holiday time and the beach was crowded with bathers and picnickers. He strode along carefully, scrutinising the smooth surface for the sign of a rise. He

muttered a prayer — or an imprecation — and lo, a fish
came up in a classic smelt rise directly in front of him. Derek
floundered into the water, elbowing aside two cavorting
children and lengthened his line to cover the rise. The smelt
fly hit the water and he started a fast retrieve. The line
tightened and he raised the straining rod high. The fish put
on a wonderful performance. An audience gathered and
there were loud cries of acclaim for the brave angler.
A coach stopped at the roadside verge and a gaggle of
American package tourists erupted to watch the action.

   By now Derek was aware of his audience and the
enthusiasm of the American visitors especially. He walked
the beaten 5-pounder up onto the beach and put down his
rod. Then he bent down, carefully unhooked the fly and
straightened up with the fish in both hands. He walked into
the water, waded out and tenderly placed the trout in its
natural element. A sudden silence fell on the observers as he
let the beautiful fish go and it wobbled off into deeper water.

   As he returned ashore, one of the American men said
unbelievingly, 'Hey Mister, why'd you put back a lunker
like that?' Derek looked at him with wide-eyed innocence.
'Why'd I put it back? We always put back little ones like that
here.' He picked up his rod and walked back to the car. In
five minutes his gear was packed away and with a wave of
his hand he started on the 380-kilometre drive back to
Wellington.

Whakamoenga

Piwakawaka - Fantail

June

Flaxbush Pool - Waitahanui

June 1

Another sortie to the Tauranga-Taupo today but very
different from last week. A lovely clear day, almost
summer-warm. Four anglers in the Crescent when we
arrived, so we back-tracked, drove south and went in
through the farm — and about nine gates — to the upper
river. It was low and we saw fish everywhere, but in the
gin-clear water they saw us too.

Laying the salmon-pink floating line onto the fast run
below the inflow of the Mangakowhitiwhiti Stream, I landed
two plump highly-coloured hen fish and a rusty old jack
slab. Below me, George fished the same Hare and Copper
nymph and took four fish one after the other in the slow
deeper run beneath the drab stand of sooty manuka.

In the Mangakowhitiwhiti Pool, working the nymphs
deep in the swirling eddies, we scored another brace each
and cast longing eyes upstream where the river twists and
curves down through the shallow gorge. Beautiful water.
Long smooth pools and swift shallows that bubble and froth

129

like champagne, but closed alas, from today until November. Beyond this point is spawning water.

Ate our lunch in the sun beside the confluence of the two streams. Two beady-eyed little fantails fussed and fluttered in the manuka close by but showed no interest in our breadcrumbs. Their flight is a series of erratic, almost spasmodic movements, hawking insects in and around the foliage. Often you hear the tiny click of the beak mandibles as they tweak flies out of mid-air.

Fished back down to the car, George with a lure and me with a small Greenwell's Glory. Five more fish were released to grow wiser. Sixteen all told and all returned. A lovely day.

June 4

Sunday, and quite a few trolling boats tracking around Whakamoenga Rocks and into Mine Bay this afternoon. Fine and mild. A good day to be out either in a boat or on shore.

Watched the ranger's launch scurrying between them, stopping each one, measuring fish and writing details on his clipboard while his mate worked the motor. He's a hard-working and conscientious fellow, like most of them. As long as you're not bending the rules you can expect nothing but helpful advice and a cheerful word.

Reminded me of the one many years ago when George first came to Taupo. He was the exception and would have been more at home in a concentration camp according to George. A big tough character, he says, and rude and arrogant with it.

Greenwell's Glory

Fishing off Acacia Bay Point one day, George saw him chivvying half a dozen boats out in the bay. Having disposed of them, he spied George on the point and set a course directly for him. Waiting until the boat was only a hundred yards off the point, George reeled in and ostentatiously crept away through the trees. The ranger shouted, George stopped

130

and when the launch came within earshot he called out, 'Anything wrong?'

'Want to see your licence,' the man shouted. 'Let's have a look at it.'

George made a great play of patting himself all over as the launch nosed in towards the rocks and eventually hauled his licence out of a back pocket. The ranger cut the motor and reached out for the licence which George held at arm's length. The boat had lost way and stood only a few feet off the rocks. George held the licence just out of reach as the ranger, alone in the boat, leaned over to grasp it. Just as his fingers closed over it George's foot slipped (he swears it was accidental) and the licence was jerked away. The ranger lunged for it, overbalanced and fell into the water with a resounding splash. The poor fellow couldn't swim and panicked loudly until George pulled him into the rocks on the end of his landing net handle.

He rubbed the unhappy man down, insisted he examine the licence, walked him to the beach and rowed him, shivering and miserable, out to his drifting boat. The man crawled soggily aboard and returned to base at Taupo.

He left only a few weeks after this unfortunate accident to be replaced by a far more amenable colleague.

June 5

George called in for a coffee today and I got him to recount the tale of the ranger to Nick, who enjoyed it enormously. She has an unkind sense of humour sometimes.

And we recalled an even earlier incumbent who held the position for many years. Johnny was a different kettle of fish altogether, a great 'character' who was well liked by all but the local evil-doers who couldn't — or wouldn't — get fish sufficient for their needs by legal means.

I'd met him a few times during his long retirement, almost always in some establishment connected with the sale and

consumption of liquor. Booze was one of the chief delights
of Johnny's life and he also had a keen eye for the ladies,
even well into his seventies. He was apprehended by a
policeman with a torch one night in highly compromising
circumstances involving a nameless lady in the back of his
old Model A Ford. At this stage he was well past his
threescore years and ten. Driving home from one of his
favourite hostelries, Johnny was always guided by a street
lamp at the end of Taupo's main thoroughfare. Here, he
knew the road bore to the left along the lake front and he
would turn the wheel accordingly, no matter what sort of a
state he was in.

One night, it was a case of the light that failed. Johnny
drove blithely on, took off from the top of the lake-edge cliff
and landed a long way down in four feet of water. He was
quite unhurt, though somewhat aggrieved, but the Model A
was never quite the same again.

He's dead now and we shan't see his like again.

June 10

Nick's birthday. Breakfast in bed — for her I mean — a
rather splendid book on herbs, and a card.

Inside the card I've written: 'Look in my fishing basket.
There are no great fish, only a few shining pebbles from the
bed of the stream, ferns from the cool green woods and wild
flowers from the places that you remember.

'I would fain console you, if I could, for the hardship of
having married an angler; a man smitten with a divine mania
who can never see a river or lake without wanting to fish in
it.

'But we have had good times together following the
stream of life to the sea. And we have passed through the
dark days without losing heart.

'So let this tell you one thing which is certain: in all the life
of your fisherman, the best piece of luck is just you.'

132

The sentiment is perfectly genuine, but I hope she never decides to browse through my copy of *Fisherman's Luck* by Henry van Dyke.

June 11

Ross arrived from Auckland last night to stay for a couple of days. He's a great fan for the Waitahanui, so bravely disregarding the temperatures, I accompanied him to the freezing river at first light this morning.

We fished the Flaxbush Pool which ran dark and cold beneath the darker overhang. I hit a fish in the lower section where it accelerates into the fast bend, but he came off after leaping once, a dim silver shape etched briefly against the black water.

Mrs Simpson

Ross swam a Mrs Simpson lure down the next pool from the opposite bank and when I crossed to join him he was fast into a good fish. It fought long and hard, helped by the strong pull of the current, but strangely made no attempt to run to the lower pool. He pumped it laboriously upstream and at last I helped it onto the frosty grass margin with my boot. A lovely fat jack, 7¼lb and in magnificent condition. Ross was delighted but cold, and so was I.

The new sun burnished the lake's calm surface as we drove home and we saw a V-formation of black swan beating ponderously up from the south over Wharewaka Point. Later, we sat with Nick in the comforting warmth of the kitchen, eating fried eggs and bacon. Outside, hanging from the big silver birch, the splendid fish rotated slowly in the sunshine.

June 12

Took Ross to Whakaipo yesterday where he hasn't fished before. Weather still fine but a sharp breeze cut in from the south-east throwing a lace of whispering foam up the beach

133

under the stark tracery of bare willow branches. The poplars too are bare, standing tall and grey above the stream mouth.

A host of starlings were screeching rustily in the poplars when we arrived. I slammed the car door and they took off as one, wheeling en masse across the bay to the eastern end with a rush of sound like a gale of wind. Why the collective noun for starlings should be a 'murmuration' I'll never know. Nothing they do is in the least like a murmur.

We drew a blank with the fish but Ross is very taken with the venue and kept trying for nearly three hours, casting a Hairy Dog into the breeze with patient determination. He gave up at last and we went home, both feeling rather chilled. Had a couple of drinks and a large dinner of roast venison, garden broad beans from the freezer together with kumara and savoy cabbage. We haven't seen Ross for a long while, so sat up late around the stove and talked beyond midnight.

He left, most unwillingly, for Auckland this morning and I spent most of the day, most unwillingly, crouched over the typewriter.

June 15

Tauhara lies black against a velvet sky tonight, untouched by the slim crescent moon and the stars.

The Lonely Mountain, despite its shape of a prone and pregnant woman, is male according to the Maori legend. Tauhara, together with Mount Taranaki, once stood at the far end of the lake with Ruapehu, Tongariro and Ngauruhoe, the Maoris say. All loved the enchanting bush-clad Pihanga, but her fierce champion was the redoubtable Tongariro.

The two most ardent would-be suitors were Taranaki and Tauhara and after a holocaust of volcanic battle, Tongariro drove away his two rivals and claimed Pihanga for his own.

Tauhara was driven to the northern end of the lake and the mighty Taranaki many more miles away to the west coast

134

near New Plymouth where it now bears the mundane name of Mount Egmont.

It seems Taranaki swore to return one day for revenge, and I'm told that no sensible Maori will live on the straight line between Taranaki and Tongariro.

Meanwhile, lonely Tauhara mourns for his lost love, uncaring for the many lights of Taupo township gathered around his feet.

June 16

The opening day of the English coarse fishing season. I always remember it, even after more than thirty years. And it always recalls old memories of lakes, ponds and rivers which, since the age of six meant only one thing to me — fish.

One of the clearest memories — naturally, I suppose — is of my first fish, a four-inch roach taken from a small Lancashire pond in my seventh year. Cupping the treasure in trembling hands, I ran breathlessly to show the prize to authority. The fish languished in a jam jar for some time, was taken home by bicycle and inevitably died a few hours later. The little silver and scarlet corpse was buried in the garden with due solemnity and a cross of twigs erected over the grave.

Another memory, poignantly clear, is of Cumberland's Lake Windermere, the venue for another holiday. This, for one newly besotted with the magic of fishing, was the ultimate apotheosis of youthful dreams. In the still dawn of a summer's day, I'd push the dinghy out from the stone jetty of the lakeside farmhouse and glide the smooth surface before lowering the anchor into the silent depths of the bay. Equipped with rudimentary rod and line and a can of bright minnows trapped the previous day from the shallows, I tempted the bold perch. The brilliant red tip of the float would bob two or three times then slide away under the surface. I'd strike against the thrilling resistance and soon the black-barred perch, spiky red dorsal extended like an alarm signal, would be drumming on the bottom boards of the boat. We ate them for breakfast with home-cured bacon and they were delicious.

Today, almost half a century later, I caught two lusty rainbow trout from Whakamoenga Rocks, both of them well over 4lb. Lovely fish, but they can't compare with the thrill of that four-inch roach or even the bold striped perch of Lake Windermere.

June 18

A cold storm thrashed the lake today, rolling heavy-shouldered waves to the south. Tauhara and the township were blanked out by moving curtains of rain and a dismal wind moaned in the pines behind the house. Rain eased this afternoon and we took the trailer to the bush for compost. Wet and cold amongst the close growth of native trees and we were glad of our oilskin parkas. Loaded up and drove back through the light drizzle. To the east, brilliant white sunlight shafted like searchlight beams through the black cloud, flooding the Kaimanawa foothills with an eerie pallor.

June 19

A resurgence of the storm last night but now coming in from the east and today was wilder again.

Two visiting Americans referred to me from a local motel insisted on trying their luck despite conditions. Drove them to Whakamoenga but fishing was out of the question with seven-foot waves slamming up and over the flat rock faces. Returned to Acacia Bay Point for a modicum of shelter but the easterly was pounding in there too. The three of us squeezed onto the point and got soaked during a difficult hour. I hooked a fish and handed the rod to the nearest man. It fought strongly for half a minute then came off.

My American felt its substance and swore it was the most powerful trout he'd ever been connected with. He was well satisfied with this small blessing. Now he had some idea of what Taupo fishing was all about, he said. Some of these people could give us a valuable lesson in the philosophy of sportsmanship.

June 23

The rather horsy-looking lady rolled out a lovely line across and down the current just below the Turangi bridge. I'd stopped the car close to the lodge on the southern side of the Tongariro bridge to watch for a few minutes as I always do if someone's fishing there.

She wore a well-cut tweed jacket, narrow-brimmed felt hat, a bright yellow stock and thigh waders. She threw the line in a smooth flat plane behind her right shoulder and punched it forward across the swift run of water, then followed the invisible lure with the rod point. Halfway down the rod dipped and came up in a jolting arc. The obliging fish forged up against the current and she let it take the loose coils of line from her left hand. When it was directly onto the reel she held hard until it turned downstream towards the tail of the pool.

I got out of the car to have a closer look and walked over the stones to the scene of battle. 'Looks like a good fish,' I called. She glanced briefly in my direction.

'Yes, not a bad sort of animal. Seen worse.' The accent was pure English southern county.

The fish now held in midstream and she waded down to get below it. It began to tire and she stepped carefully backwards out of the water, forcing it to follow. 'Now here's what I want you to do,' she called over her shoulder.

Jock Scott

'I shall bring it in down there in that shallow run and I want you to tail it as soon as you get the chance.'

'Why certainly,' I replied. 'Glad to be of assistance.'

She glanced at me again. 'None of that kicking it out, mind you. I've seen too much of that sort of carry-on here and I don't like it.'

'Absolutely not,' I promised and took up station close to the water's edge. The lady regained more line, retreated further back up the stones and steered the beaten fish into the shallows. Shipping a bit of river over my shoes, I reached across and circled the wrist of the tail between thumb and forefinger and lifted it out, a handsome fresh-run 5-pounder.

The horsy lady pointed to a small patch of sand well away from the water. 'Just put it down there like a good chap. Must say you did that rather well. A fishing man, obviously.'

I did as directed. She laid her rod down carefully and bent to unhook the fish. The fly looked like a small English salmon pattern, bright and garish against the grey stones.

'Salmon fly, isn't it?' I asked. She nodded. 'Jock Scott. Always use 'em here. That's my first today but I killed three brace on it yesterday. Well, thanks for your help, very civil of you.' She bent over the fish again, rapping it smartly between the eyes with a small rock.

Realising I'd been dismissed I walked back to the car, squelching wetly in my soaking shoes. As I drove across the bridge she waded into the stream once more, expertly shooting line to cover the middle water.

June 26

Perseverance through a cold hour on Acacia Bay Point last night won me a fine 5½lb brownie.

We invited him to dinner tonight — a most welcome guest stuffed with breadcrumbs, chopped onions, herbs and seasoning and strips of lemon peel. Couldn't manage the

138

whole lot so we took the tail portion to old Bob up the road who's very partial to this sort of thing.

Brownies are the exception in the average Taupo angler's bag although they form twenty to twenty-five percent of the trout population here. They're a more subtle fish than the rainbow, harder to catch and usually taken only after dark in this area. But we do get a few on the nymph in the rivers during daylight. I like to catch them because of their relative rarity and more suspicious nature. Few Taupo anglers consider them worthy of special attention, but in the South Island, and in other parts of the North Island, they're appreciated for the quality of fishing they provide. Many years ago I caught an 18½-pounder in a South Island lake. It was the only fish two of us took in two days' fishing and fifty minutes passed between hooking and landing.

Some years later, as a guest in a central North Island fishing lodge, I saw a plaster cast of an 11½lb rainbow caught by the proprietress, a lady noted for her angling prowess and lack of tact and diplomacy. 'That's a lovely fish,' I remarked to her after dinner one night.

'Yes, not bad is it?' she replied. 'You ever catch a trout that size?'' I admitted to the 18½-pounder. Her face fell briefly then she fixed me with a gimlet eye. 'Rainbow or brown?' I told her the truth of the matter and her face lightened again. 'Oh that's nothing for a brownie,' she said.

This put me back in my place all right but I still feel no shame.

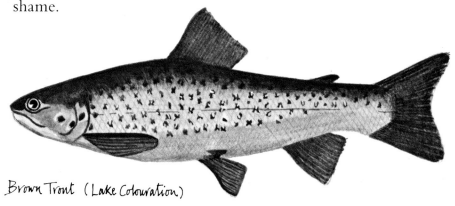

Brown Trout (Lake Colouration)

June 29

Sleet-laced wind from the north today, whispering coldly through the bare tops of the Whakaipo poplars.

The top gate padlocked for some reason or other so had to leave the car and walk down to the lake. A brilliant cock-pheasant exploded out of the roadside scrub with a startling dry clatter of wings. Frightened the life out of me and almost wished I had a shotgun. Brodie nearly had a heart attack too, but recovered quickly to burst into a frenzy of barking as the bird disappeared into the trees.

It wasn't worth the walk down really, nor the long haul back. We spent two hours without a touch and even Brodie seemed a little bored. Her spirits rose on the way back when she came on a family of quail around a bend in the track. They gave her quite a good run before taking to the air. I often wonder what she'd do if she ever caught up with one. She'd be painfully embarrassed, I'm sure.

July

Admirals Pool - Tongariro River

July 1

Another family has moved in close by. The evergreen virgilia has a nest in it already and the new tenants are busily to-ing and fro-ing with bits of this and that to complete the accommodation for an early brood of youngsters.

The song thrush is one of the earliest breeders, sometimes starting construction in mid or even early June. While they were away about their business today I climbed up to have a look and was surprised to find the nest just about complete. The outer case is woven twigs and grass stalks, carefully plastered with mud, and the inside a smooth cup of wood pulp bound with, I think, saliva.

Dropped a few moribund snails from the rockery close to the virgilia this afternoon. A couple of hours later they were gone, and I don't believe Herman or Brodie ate them. We'll have to keep a close eye on Herman. His ornithological interests don't extend to conservation of the species.

July 6

'I don't know what they'd think at home if they could see the way I fish here,' Peter told me over a glass of beer today.

He's not long out from Britain, retired after an illustrious army career spanning nearly forty years. He and his wife spend most of their time fishing and cultivating their magnificent garden, an acre of richly supplemented volcanic soil close to the township. My inferiority complex takes on a further dimension whenever I see it.

Peter's fishing experience in Britain was mainly on the verdant water meadows of the Test and Itchen valleys in Hampshire where the dry fly, and sometimes the nymph, is the only acceptable method for a gentleman, but while he delights in the nymph and dry fly fishing available in the Taupo area, he also enjoys fishing the sunken lure in both lake and rivers. Smelting, especially, is one of his favourite techniques in the season.

The use of the wet or sunken fly on the hallowed waters of the Test and Itchen brands a man with the mark of the beast — definitely persona non grata with the local purists to whom the dry fly is sacrosanct. Nymph fishing is grudgingly tolerated in some parts.

Peter told me of a young acquaintance given the opportunity to fish a stretch of the Test through the good offices of a relative. The young fellow apparently had little respect for the local traditions and after a fruitless hour or so with the dry fly, resorted to the criminal heresy of fishing a sunken fly downstream.

He had two fish hitched to the loop of one thigh wader (another peccadillo quite unacceptable to the purists) when he was spotted from afar by a retired high court judge who was a dry fly man to the marrow.

'How are you getting on?' the ancient jurist shouted.

Mistaking the query for, 'What are you getting them on?' the young man called back, 'Wet fly.'

The other's face fell for a moment, then, refusing to

believe the unbelievable, cheerfully replied, 'Never mind. Happens to me sometimes if I wade too deep!'

July 9

A grey and lowering day with intermittent rain but not so cold. Did some more 'muck-spreading' — good old horse manure dug well in and top-dressed with a mulch of bush compost. It worked like a charm with the sweet corn this last summer when some of the plants topped eight feet. If I really feed up the soil they crop wonderfully well, even sown as close as seven inches apart.

The native bush on the point and beyond remains dark and matt green, but the willow branches are turning dull burnt-orange. On the near point a few tenacious leaves cling to the poplars and a sad wind bends their skeletal tops to the south.

July 12

Bright and cold again with mist lying low until well on in the morning. My father's birthdate. The anniversary of the Battle of the Boyne, as he invariably used to remind us.

I don't believe he was ever in Ireland and regarded the race with a somewhat irrational suspicion as a flippant and contrary lot. Wonder what he'd have thought about his younger son having married one. Initial dismay, I'm sure, but equally sure Nick would have charmed the bias out of him in short order.

Thinking of that recalled my second trip to Ireland many years ago, when the engine driver to whom I'd talked fishing before departure from Belfast, stopped the train halfway across the country to show me one of his favourite salmon pools on the Shannon. We left the train and walked down to the river a quarter-mile away. Here was where he stood to throw his fly into the deep run under the far bank. Over there he'd landed a handsome fresh-run fish only last month.

I can still see the line of indignant faces framed by the windows of the train as we ambled back to continue the interrupted journey. I buried my face in a magazine for the rest of the trip. Nothing was said, but I felt my fellow passengers' eyes boring through the flimsy barricade all the way to our destination.

July 14

Caught no fish from my little bay along from the Mapara Stream mouth today. Another misty calm and should have known better than to try, but it was delightful nonetheless. Sat on the fallen willow trunk smoking a cigarette and watching the water and the sky. The sun sucked up the mist, unveiling the bluffs on the far side of the bay where the high rough pasture merges into scrub. Maybe a breeze will come soon, I thought. But it didn't, so I waded slowly back.

Saw a bundle of white feathers wedged amongst the underwater roots of a big willow. A red-billed gull, hopelessly entangled by heavy monofilament nylon. Head and neck hung loose, crimson mandibles agape, flaccidly rolling with the movement at the water's edge in a grotesque, slow-motion parody of life.

July 18

I can never clearly recall the exact moment of the strike. Fishing a dry fly or even a sunken nymph there's usually a visual factor which impinges on the memory. The dry fly disappears as it's sucked down in the ring of the rise; the take of the nymph is signalled by an arresting of the moving line or the sudden dive of your indicator. But with a sunken lure, unless in very shallow water, only the tactile senses are involved.

Landed a fine 4lb hen fish from Wharewaka Point this morning and she gave me something to remember for ten or twelve minutes. But I can't clearly recall the moment of the strike. Pity, because for me this is the apotheosis of the whole business, the moment of truth. Even the ultimate landing of the fish isn't in the same category as far as I'm concerned.

Looking back on it now — even moments after the event — I want to know exactly what I felt and thought. After loosely coiling in against the minimal pull of line and lure, the shock of sudden heavy resistance jerks me into immediate physical response. What happens in the mind? The signal from brain to hand short-circuits the memory and the magic moment is lost in retrospect.

I'm not complaining really, just curious. The 4-pounder, filleted and quick-fried in seasoned butter, satisfied all senses.

July 20

Wedding anniversary. Haven't forgotten it yet and Nick was delighted with the feather-light mohair scarf from the local craft shop. She didn't forget either, and I'm still wearing the fisherman's waistcoat with its innumerable pockets, loops, zips, tapes and even a sort of small knapsack attachment on the back. It's lined with nylon wool and has a woollen collar with a plastic parka hood folded back inside. Had dinner in town with one and half bottles of good German wine. An excellent day.

July 22

Cold as charity on the point today. Only lasted an hour and came back fishless, chilled to the bone in spite of shirt, sweater, new waistcoat and oilskin parka. The smell of rain on the wind but it hasn't come yet. Had a long hot shower and packed the stove with chunks of manuka. It's far better than pine, burns longer and throws out much more heat. George's electric sawbench is a godsend. Hope he never builds his own smokehouse.

July 23

Brodie's big day. The first full-scale dog show held in Taupo. She was hardly a ball of self-confidence and exemplified the description 'hand dog' to a tee when confronted with a bewildering assortment of canine shapes and sizes.

Cool, calm and noble she was not, but managed to win a green ribbon all the same. We didn't have the heart to tell her it was for being the only Scottie in the show.

July 25

The nights draw in quickly now and it's often dark by four o'clock. Hardly light by seven in the morning so a dawn fishing sortie allows a relatively decent lie-in.

Shivering waist deep in Te Kumi Bay this morning at six-thirty, watching a cold grey pallor creep unwillingly above the Kaimanawas. Twice something grabbed the Hairy Dog and let go immediately. Then there was nothing for a long time. An hour and a half was enough. Close furled cloud banking up from the south showed no signs of a break and I guessed there'd be no sun all day. A fish latched onto the fly as I reeled in and a seven-inch monster almost shot over my shoulder. It had engulfed the lure with gourmand enthusiasm and the hook point protruded behind one eye. Had to kill it to extract the hook and that put me in a bad mood. Spent most of the day writing but it wasn't a success and I'll have to go over it all again.

July 26

There's the odd deer not far from home but the local spotlighters usually clean them up before real stalkers get to them. Sometimes we hear a few shots at night when the wind's in the right quarter, but there's been nothing now for a few weeks.

Took the 30-06 up the hill behind Jerusalem Bay before first light today. Black and miserable but not too cold. Halfway through the manuka flats the torch beam picked out a paunch and pair of forelegs beside the track. A few yards away I saw (and smelt) the fly-blown head of a young hind. Only a few days old so the spot-lighters seem to have been here after all. Climbed up through the cutover stands of pine to the top of the ridge overlooking Mine Bay just in time to see a cold white wash of light lifting in the east. A fitful wind moaned in the high scrub and I eased down to a sheltered bench covering the faint track far below.

Sat there for an hour watching the open stretch of track as the rising sun warmed the dark gully. Beyond the next ridge, Mine Bay shone silver grey between the encircling arms of bush. Lay down on the flat outcrop, positioned the rifle and waited.

After nine o'clock when I saw a movement I wasn't really expecting. Felt myself trembling as the red stag stepped warily out of the shadows more than 150 yards below.

Couldn't count the tines but he was probably a ten-pointer. Beamed the 'scope onto him, following the slow and hesitant gait. He stopped briefly and I centred the cross-hairs on the spine where the neck joined the thick shoulders.

When I looked up after the echoing blast he was gone and two hinds raced across the clearing and disappeared. Bruised and breathless from sliding and tumbling down the gully face, I cast around for signs of a hit. But there was nothing — no hair, no blood, just fresh prints in the mud and pumice of the track.

Waited ten minutes to get my breath, then started the weary climb back to the top of the ridge. Just as well we have the odd bit of venison and wild pork still in the freezer.

July 29

Just wish it was smelting time again, but that's almost half a year away. Looking out across the cold wind-scoured lake it's hard to imagine the sun warm on the bright water and the trout slashing into the shining hordes close under the greening willows.

The smelt are there of course, way down in the deeps where they'll stay until the spawning urge draws them to the shallow margins of the lake in late November or December.

But there are many compensations despite the steely grip of winter. Not least the comfort and security of home after time spent in the outer world, and the welcoming warmth of a wood-burning stove. Brodie is far more lively at this time of year, but Herman sensibly makes sure he doesn't overtax his strength and spends most of the day in Brodie's basket.

Puriri

August

Cliff Pool - Tongariro River

August 4

Helped George demolish three big dead manuka from the scrub along Mapara Road today. His chainsaw made short work of the trimming and we heaved them onto the trailer and cut them to size on his electric sawbench. Took home a full trailer-load of chunks for the stove and a rubbish bag of sawdust for the smoker.

George's neighbours were glad when we'd finished I'm sure, but how much worse for us having to stand right over the infernal machine! My ears are still ringing from the shriek of the saw biting through the hard trunk. Still no rain but heavy cloud building up from the south this evening.

August 5

Rain came last night and continued today, laced with sleet from the cold southern peaks. The manuka logs spit and pop behind the glass doors of the stove tonight and Brodie lies close with her feet in the air, long nose and eyelids twitching spasmodically as she pursues some hapless dream victim to its doom. Herman sits hunched in Brodie's basket, white elbows poking through the soft grey fur, paws neatly folded under his chest. The yellow slitted eyes gaze unblinking into the glowing stove. His mind obviously elsewhere too. Probably away with the birds.

August 7

Red Setter

Cold, cold, cold. Only fishermen, hunters and lunatics leave a warm bed in the freezing dawn when they don't have to. But I had this silly idea yesterday of bringing home a fresh-run Tongariro fish for today's breakfast. The river has fined down after the rain, my spies told me, and a run of fish moved up from the lake.

At six this morning the grass above the river crunched underfoot and only the icy stars witnessed my madness. The Breakfast Pool ran pewter grey as I stepped in opposite the big rock at the head. The Red Setter lure swept across and down three times without a touch. The fourth time I held it pulsing in the current at the end of its run, twitching the line in my hand to liven it. A heavy pull told me someone else was up and about. We sorted out our differences in the darkness but it was hard work for us both. Had to regain the casting line and half the backing from a powerful run almost into the head of the Major Jones Pool.

An uphill battle fighting the river's pull as well, but at last I worked the fish in close and eased her up onto the gravel with my boot. A lovely hen, sleek and silver in the torchlight, with only the barest suggestion of a roseate bar along the flank. Killed and gutted her on the spot and the blood showed black and dense on the stones.

When I looked up, a pale and luminous duck-egg green had lifted the darkness in the east. Walked back to the car, the 4½lb fish dangling wetly from one finger. The other fingers were freezing too and I had a job fumbling the key into the ignition.

150

An hour later, the two orange-pink fillets whispered together in the frying pan with a slice of bacon in between them. I was warm and didn't feel at all like a lunatic. We ground black pepper and sprinkled salt over them. Hooray for the Breakfast Pool!

August 10

The big virgilia is now a 'family tree'. Climbed onto the roof last week to look into the nest and saw mother bedded well down in the cup. She watched me with a beady suspicious eye, moving never a muscle for ten long minutes.

Climbed down again and waited for half an hour until she left the nest for food which didn't seem to be forthcoming from her husband. This time from the roof I saw the four pale blue eggs nestled in the warm cup. Today the eggs are gone and three grotesque thick-lipped heads gape expectantly to the sky. I can even hear a faint high squeaking like mice under the floor. In all the animal world, birds must have the ugliest babies. Searched carefully below the tree but could find no trace of the fourth egg.

August 12

A splendid powder-blue day. Quite a bite in the air but it didn't take long to work up a mild sweat digging over the sweet corn patch. I'd left the stalks to rot down but they haven't made much progress so I chopped them up small with the slasher and added them to the compost bin. Wish I had one of those machines which grind vegetation to a fine consistency. Compost rots down so much more quickly in small pieces. What wonderful clarity in the air at this time of year. Even Ngauruhoe, eighty kilometres away, stands out bold and clear — much closer it seems than seen through the soft haze of a summer's day.

August 13

Roy blooded his new carbon fibre rod today at Whakamoenga. What a beautiful little weapon. Only seven-and-a-half feet long with a remarkably small diameter right down to the cork. It weighs a feather-light three-and-a-half ounces and throws a No. 7 line with ease. He tells me it can handle anything from a No. 4 to a No. 8 line without complaint.

Tried it out myself for a while and astounded by the power in such a light and frail-looking wand. Later, it hooked and landed a splendid 4¾-pounder for Roy with no trouble at all. But it cost well over $200. Think I might wait a while for mine.

August 15

Parsons Glory

The constraints of winter are not always so hard to bear. We launched the two-seater fibreglass kayak from the beach this morning, sliding easily over the mirror surface of the bay towards the long green arm of the second point. The double paddle pushed us along at a great pace, water popping and bubbling under the narrow prow.

Handed the paddle to Nick not far from the point and pitched the Parsons Glory just short of the flat pancake rocks under the willows. It sank for a few moments while Nick back-paddled gently to keep way on. The shifting dapple of light flickered under the willows close in, but further out the sun's glare bounced up into our eyes from the calm water. Nick stroked the light shell around the point in reverse while I tweaked the line spasmodically to liven the deep-working lure. Looking cautiously over the side I could see the weed-mottled floor of the lake slipping past twelve or fourteen feet below. It was hot now and I wished I'd brought my polaroids. Suddenly the rod point dipped and the reel screamed its urgent falsetto. Held the rod high, watching the line rise in the water before a fish shattered the

152

smooth surface fifty feet away. Nick rested her paddle and the fish sounded, pulling the stem of the kayak slowly around and out into the bay.

The combined weight of the boat and the rod's spring soon decided the contest. I dipped with the landing net and dropped it between my knees in the bottom of the boat where the ripe 3-pounder splattered water all over my trousers. Upended the net in the water and she streaked away for the bottom, leaving three carnelian eggs slowly sinking in her wake.

We made across to the further side of the bay where George and Muriel's lawn comes down almost to the water. As we came abreast we saw the pair of them sitting under the beach umbrella on the stone patio. On the table were what looked like two bottles of beer. George got up and beckoned us in. It would have been churlish to refuse.

Clematis

August 18

Nick away doing her radio session this morning so I got out the Beethoven 'Pastoral', shut all the doors and windows and turned it up full throttle. Can't stand 'pop' music at this pitch but Beethoven's something different. The whole house shaking to the 'thunderstorm' passage when I heard a faint knocking through the reverberant percussion and sounding brass. Not Fate knocking at the door, surely?

No. Jim and Marianne were standing on the doorstep mouthing inaudibly. Waved them inside and went to turn down the record. 'Good God,' Jim complained, 'we could hear it at the bottom of the road even in the car!'

I told them I liked to get the full feeling and didn't think anyone heard if doors and windows were shut. Jim rolled his eyes at Marianne and said he wanted a beer.

Almost through the second bottle when Nick came back and she listened to a further recapitulation of their skiing weekend on Ruapehu. They're not due back in Wellington until Tuesday so they've decided to stay the night. Had a great old natter and finished off their bottle of medicinal Scotch. It's late now and Jim at least is sleeping well by the sound of it. Frankly, I prefer Beethoven.

August 19

Down to the point for an hour this morning, hoping for a fish Jim and Marianne could take back with them. No joy so we dug one out of the freezer instead. Jim loves to eat trout but considers fishing a bore.

August 21

Baby song-thrushes seem to be doing well and almost double the size since I first saw them ten days ago. Suddenly remembered the opossums yesterday and recalled that they sometimes take baby birds from a nest, so nailed a collar of thin sheet aluminium a couple of feet up the virgilia's trunk. They'll get no purchase for their claws on that.

In bed last night remembered the one leaping from the roof to the virgilia some months ago and started worrying about that. Not long before I imagined a sound on the roof and got up to investigate. Nothing there of course, and the freezing night air almost took my breath away, but stayed for a moment or so. A full moon, huge and white and cold,

154

sailed high above the southern mountains, burnishing the lake silver bright. To the north, beyond sleeping Tauhara, plumes of thermal steam hung like ghostly pillars in the still air.

Kotukutuku - Tree Fuschia

August 23

Cold still. Low grey sky pressing down with no light relief all day. Packed the stove this morning and spent half an hour chopping more kindling. Brodie helps by trying to catch the pieces as they fall from the block, yelping impatiently if I'm too slow. Herman has no time for such foolishness but watches benignly from a window. He wisely hurries the cold weather along by remaining unconscious for the greater part of each day. If I had the choice, I'd opt for being a cat in my next reincarnation. A spoilt one, of course — Herman is the ideal model.

August 24

Still cold and grey with a deceptive light wind that cuts to the bone. Braved Whakamoenga Rocks before lunch and fished for an hour without a touch.

A sudden burst of activity at one o'clock with three fish and two more strikes within twenty minutes. Then nothing. Kept one fish which we had for dinner tonight. Cut it into steaks, rolled in seasoned flour then dipped them in beaten egg before frying for five minutes. Tartare sauce, with nasturtium seeds instead of capers, bottled beans from the garden and hard golden chips that clinked on the plates. Fish and chips with a difference.

August 27

Weather improving today, even a clear sunrise with cloud falling away to the south. Saw it to best advantage from the hill behind the house first thing this morning.

Didn't have to wait at all but saw the rabbit hunched on the frosted grass by the fenceline as I topped the rise. He saw me too, the last thing he ever saw and flopped without a twitch when the Hornet took him through the neck. A young buck in beautiful winter condition. There was no apparent mark on the body when I went to pick him up, only a small jewel of bright blood at the nose.

Had an interested audience of two while I cleaned the rabbit on the block. Brodie claimed the two back feet and went off to bury them after a decent period of worrying and chewing. Herman, ever practical, sat quietly until the liver came his way, then sloped off purposefully under the house. I slit open the belly with the razor knife, cut down inside each leg, severed the tail and eased out the evil-smelling viscera. Worked the skin off the back legs, cut through the neck then pulled the whole skin off like a glove. It's not my favourite occupation so I rarely shoot more than one or two at a time. Very rarely able to, anyway.

August 29

John has that Tongariro feeling he said on the phone today. All right with me I told him, but not another dawn patrol so soon after the last one. Agreed on a more or less civilised start at eight-thirty or so and it would be the upper river with the nymph.

Weather much improved now but cold still. Sat up late tying half-a-dozen Hare and Copper nymphs with an extra turn or two of copper wire to get them down through the fast water.

156

A sharp clear morning with the Tongariro in fine order. Dropped our bags and waders on the stones by Harry's rock above the Cliff Pool and began to tackle up.

Rubber doesn't take long to warm even in the winter sun and the baby mallard seemed very comfortable when John bent down to pick up his waders. We chucked him under the chin and stroked the downy poll. 'Well I'm sorry,' John said, 'but I want to put them on.' He lifted the tiny creature carefully and placed it on a rock, then struggled into the waders and made for the tail of the pool. The duckling followed. By the time he had his first cast on the water, the duckling had taken up station beside his right wader paddling manfully against the current to hold position.

I went in level with the rock and began to cast the nymph upstream. Twice the suck of the rapids proved too much for the duckling's strength and his protector floundered downstream to retrieve him and place him on a rock for safe-keeping. But he wouldn't be safely kept. Further upstream where the pull of the current eased, the little bird rode high and confident beside him. Despite the handicap, John hooked and landed a fine 4-pounder. He rapped it on the head and we stood back to admire the prize. The duckling swaggered up and mounted the cold flank with a proprietary air.

'Well Mum,' I said, 'I'll work up from the tail now and you and the family carry on from here.'

Looking back with a self-satisfied smirk, I saw the duckling making towards me helped along by shooing motions from his treacherous foster-mother. Stepping up the pace I reached the tail of the pool and looked back. The duckling was nowhere to be seen. Two casts later I looked down to see him paddling strenuously beside me. He looked up with a knowing air.

Within moments I struck a fish which bored up strongly towards the big rock. A sudden urgent cheeping turned my head and I saw the duckling in the fast water losing way rapidly. I turned back to the fish which was surging up to the head of the pool and looked back again. The little bird was coming to the edge of the white water and calling incessantly.

'Oh damn it all to hell!' I shouted. Struggling ashore I propped the rod amongst the stones and lumbered off downstream. But I was too late. Bobbing like a cork in the foam, the duckling was well on his way downriver. I watched until he was out of sight, then turned slowly back upstream. Naturally enough my fish was gone.

'It was all your damn fault,' I told John. 'Why didn't you observe your responsibilities?'

He spread his hands. 'Is it my fault if you look more like a female duck than me? Anyway, don't worry about it. Those things are unsinkable, he'll come to no harm. He might even be back shortly.'

I flinched. 'Either that,' John said, 'or he'll find his mother again.' He smiled unkindly. 'Just like your fish — he's probably back with his mum now too.'

August 31

A great day yesterday and today was a real cracker too. Almost have the feeling that winter is giving ground. After all, tomorrow is officially the first day of spring.